PRAISE FOR
PARENTING

"Do you ever wish you had a parenting [...]
share the mistakes they made as a paren[...] [...]
those same pitfalls? Now you do! Jonathan McKee offers timeless
wisdom for parents who want to look back on their kids' childhood
someday and honestly say they have no regrets."

—Jim Daly, President—Focus on the Family

"Every parenting book from Jonathan McKee is a gem, and this one is
no exception. Combining his own experience with what other parents
have said they wish they had done differently, he clearly presents better
ways to lead and connect with your kids, at any age."

—Shaunti Feldhahn, Social Researcher, National Speaker,
and Bestselling Author of *For Women Only* and *For Parents Only*

"*If I Had a Parenting Do-Over* is a challenging and yet hopeful book.
Jonathan shares honest examples of how he would 'do over' certain
elements of his parenting, but also graciously offers positive strategies
and suggestions that we all can learn from. As a parent of three kids, I
am grateful for Jonathan's stories, practical tips, and helpful research.
This book is a gem."

—Sean McDowell, Ph.D., Biola University Professor, Speaker,
and Author of Over Fifteen Books including *A New Kind of Apologist*

"If I Had a Parenting Do-Over is an eye-opening exploration into the
parenting practices many of us settle for, only to look back in regret.
The 7 vital changes Jonathan proposes are insightful, packed with the
wisdom that only comes through experience, and grounded in research.
I highly recommend this book to any parent."

—Doug Fields, Author, and Creator of IntentionalParenting.com

"I don't know any moms and dads who feel like they parented perfectly.
Not one! In fact, I know countless parents who look back in hindsight
and wish they could change a few things. That's where Jonathan McK-
ee's book is so practical, providing 20/20 hindsight from hundreds of
parents on what they'd do differently 'if they had a parenting do-over.'"

—Jeff & Cheryl Scruggs, Authors of *I Do Again*,
and Founders of Hope Matters Marriage Ministries

"I love how Jonathan McKee communicates. This book is practical, hopeful, and absolutely relevant. I have probably spent too much time in my life thinking about how I would have parented our kids differently. This book gave me helpful perspective."

—Jim Burns, PhD, President of HomeWord, and Author of
Confident Parenting and *Teaching Your Children Healthy Sexuality*

"Wow, did this book bring back memories of rearing two teenage boys. I was right there with 'City Slickers' wanting a do-over myself. McKee crafts scenarios from his own family that hit the mark, backed up with current research in the area of parent-child relations and communications. This is one of the books that all expecting families should get before they 'open the package.' The seven vital changes are great advice for parenting and also valuable in other areas of life and relationships. A must-read!"

—Dudley Chancey, PhD, Professor of Youth & Family Ministry, Oklahoma Christian University; Executive Director of National Conference on Youth Ministries and Director of Winterfest.org Youth Conferences

"Do-Overs are great—but what if you could do it right the first time? We all makes mistakes, and often learn best from them, but a mistake avoided is always preferred. This little book can help you do just that—learn from the mistakes of others. Loaded with simple themes, great stories, and practical tips, this book will help any parent do it right the first time! Refreshing, fun and insightful. . .it is worth the time for any parent to check out this book."

—Pastor Karl Bastian, "The Kidologist," Founder of Kidology.org

"The noise of technology makes parenting harder than ever before. And most parents feel like they are navigating an unprecedented journey. That's where Jonathan's book is so unique. Jonathan provides real-world help based on 20/20 hindsight from literally hundreds of parents. Jonathan's wisdom and experience make this a must-have book for any young parent, including me!"

—Curt Steinhorst, National Speaker and Author

IF I HAD A
PARENTING

DO
OVER

7 VITAL CHANGES I'D MAKE

Author and youth culture expert Jonathan McKee
gets real about **what worked**. . . and **what didn't work**. . .
in his own parenting

Jonathan McKee

SHILOH RUN  PRESS
An Imprint of Barbour Publishing, Inc.

Print ISBN 978-1-68322-067-1

eBook Editions:
Adobe Digital Edition (.epub) 978-1-68322-164-7
Kindle and MobiPocket Edition (.prc) 978-1-68322-165-4

Cover design: Greg Jackson, Thinkpen Design

The author is represented by, and this book is published in association with, the literary agency of WordServe Literary Group, Ltd., www.wordserveliterary.com.

Published by Shiloh Run Press, an imprint of Barbour Publishing, Inc., P.O. Box 719, Uhrichsville, Ohio 44683, www.shilohrunpress.com.

Our mission is to publish and distribute inspirational products offering exceptional value and biblical encouragement to the masses.

Member of the
Evangelical Christian
Publishers Association

Printed in the United States of America.

CONTENTS

ACKNOWLEDGMENTS

I can't possibly write about do-overs without thanking the one person who makes a fresh start truly possible, my Lord Jesus Christ, the architect of new beginnings.

I have to thank my family and give them credit for enduring through much of the pain in this book. By its nature, an exposition about parenting regrets is made possible only when an imperfect parent has messed up and then realized his or her mistakes. This means my family had to endure said mistakes while I learned the hard way. So what I really need to say is, "I'm sorry," foremost to Alec, my oldest, and then to my girls, Alyssa and Ashley. Please forgive me. My hope is that other parents will heed my warnings and avoid these same mistakes!

Thank you to all who were part of the research going into this book. Thanks to my blog readers, those of you attending my parenting workshops where I specifically asked you questions about your biggest parenting regrets, and the countless friends whom I e-mailed and asked the question directly. Your answers made me realize I was not alone in my regrets, or in my desire to parent better.

Thanks to the handful of you who took the time to read early drafts of this book, share your honest reactions, and make comments and suggestions. Thanks to Carolyn Sutter, Sande Quattlebaum, Curt Steinhorst, Amy McKee, Becky Martin, John Stone, Karol Boyd, John Mah, Layton Dutton, Mark Pickham, Chris Pannell, Tim Medley, Ryan Davis, Matt Erickson, Jonathan McDuffie, Ben Palm, Alex Tufano, Barbara Straub, Chad Feight, Cathie Mackin,

Carol Lindberg, Kathie Barkow, and my parents, Tom and Susie McKee.

Thanks, Kelly and Shay over at Barbour Publishing! You two are rock stars. I hope to do many more books with you!

Thanks to my agent, Greg Johnson. I appreciate your encouragement and feedback through this project.

And thank you, Nermel the Squirrel (yes, I named him). You were constant entertainment day after day as I sat on the back patio and wrote most of this book. I wish I had your speed and agility, you fluffy little rascal!

WHERE I MESSED UP

I've never met a parent who doesn't regret certain parenting decisions.

Think about it. Do you have a perfectly clean slate as a parent, or are there certain moments you wish you could just. . .erase?

Sadly, I can recall plenty of these moments, experiences I wish I could go back and try again, a little more equipped this time around. I'm the perfect example of an *imperfect* parent.

There were times I tried too hard, and times I didn't do enough. I remember countless instances when I said too much, and a few times when I said too little. I recall working long hours and then attempting to justify my neglect of my family. In contrast, I remember interfering when I should have just let my kids feel the consequences of their own actions and learn independence. My mistakes were on both ends of the spectrum.

Then there were times when I just messed up and allowed my temper to get the best of me—embarrassing moments, when I really think about it. Honestly, I can remember the expressions on the faces of my kids when I was "correcting" them. And now I ask myself: Did those moments leave emotional scars? Are my children less equipped to handle conflict in a healthy way because of Dad's anger?

If only I had a do-over.

Learning from My Mistakes

I'm a pretty introspective guy. If I mess up, I want to know not only why I messed up but how to avoid that mess-up again. (Maybe it's just because I've had so much practice at messing up!)

Introspectiveness has been an interesting personality trait for me to possess as a parent who also happens to study teenagers and parenting as a profession. My books and articles almost serve as a written record of my mistakes. "Don't try this—it will backfire every time!"

In my parenting workshops I'd be authentic whenever someone asked a question.

"Jonathan, do you have your sixteen-year-old's passwords, and do you check her phone?"

I'd answer, "Yes, and she hates it! I'm wondering if it does any good. The verdict's still out on that one."

But then I'd always add, "Here's what the experts say. The American Academy of Pediatrics recommends parents monitor their kids' media use and co-view entertainment. Common Sense Media recommends the same, but they are pretty clear that spying doesn't do any good. After all, we need to help our kids learn to make good decisions on their own. So here's how I've tried to apply all this in my home. . . ."

This balance of research and experience has been an interesting mix. I probably don't have to tell you there's a huge difference between knowledge and practice. In other words, I might read an article from a pediatrician with helpful parenting tips, but when I tried to apply these principles with my own kids, in my own house, flavored by my own shortcomings. . .the result wasn't always textbook.

Parenting is rarely textbook!

Parenting has a *huge* learning curve!

Parenting requires constantly learning and adapting.

So that's what I did. Whenever I messed up, I took note and made small tweaks.

- My son didn't respond well when I lectured him so long. I'll try a shorter lecture next time.
- Nope. . .still didn't work. Lecturing doesn't work. Period! Research reveals questions are more effective. I'll try asking questions.
- Yep. Questions worked way better. But maybe next time I need to think about my approach with the questions. I need to come off as truly curious, not like a parole officer.

These notes and observations slowly morphed my actions as a parent. My reactions changed, my disciplines changed, and even some of my rules changed.

For example, my curfew for my oldest at age sixteen was way earlier than my curfew for my youngest at the same age. Why? Because I thought an early curfew would help me keep watch over him better. Sadly, my archetypal style of helicopter parenting did exactly what research reveals—it caused rebellion. I passed up some great opportunities to give him real-world experience in decision making. I was making most decisions for him when he was in the house. I rarely asked him, "What do you think you should do?"

Don't get me wrong. My wife, Lori, and I spent countless hours passing on our morals and values. I can give you all kinds of examples:

- We read the Bible together as a family.
- We attended church regularly.
- We read devotionals, even ones specifically geared to help kids answer the question, "What would you do in this situation?"

But what I slowly began realizing I lacked was providing my kids with opportunities for real-world decision making in real-life situations. In other words, when my first two kids asked me if they could hang out with a certain friend or play a particular video game, the answer was usually yes or no. I rarely asked, "What do you think you should do?"

My kids are now eighteen, twenty, and twenty-three as I sit and write this. Looking back, I wish I had given my first two more opportunities to make decisions.

I wish I had given them more opportunities to fail.

I wish I could do it over again.

Sadly, we often learn a lot of lessons the hard way parenting our oldest kids. Then we adjust and adapt our parenting of our younger children.

My kids can definitely attest to that. My older two will be quick to say, "Why does Ashley get to do that? We never got to do that!"

Lori and I adapted our parenting.

Apparently we're not alone.

Common Regrets

When Lori and I found ourselves adapting and changing our parenting style, we began dialoguing with others about this phenomenon. We quickly discovered it's a common occurrence. Most parents look back at the outcomes of past parenting decisions and, unhappy with the results, make adjustments for the future.

The intriguing part of this whole equation was the stigma that seemed to go along with these changes or adaptations. Most parents don't advertise, "Here's where I messed up!"

It's embarrassing!

So they keep it to themselves. Sadly, their silence keeps other parents from learning from their mistakes.

So I began searching for settings where parents felt safe getting vulnerable with one another, sharing mistakes and asking for prayer and counsel. In my travels I encountered numerous churches offering parenting classes or small groups where moms and dads felt safe to open up and ask questions. Most of these venues stimulated others to share similar struggles, and even humble advice: "Here's what I learned."

People were hungry for this kind of counsel. I know I was. I loved hearing wisdom from more experienced parents, and this prompted me to begin asking: "If you could go back in time and change one parenting practice, what would you change?"

That's the question I've been asking people over the last year.

I've asked my readers about it; I've polled parents, particularly empty nesters; and I've questioned countless parents face-to-face at my workshops. The results have been eye-opening to me, not only as someone who researches parenting and youth culture but as a fellow parent!

It didn't take long for me to begin noticing common denominators. As I began documenting all my polls and surveys, the same struggles and regrets kept floating to the surface. Parents all across the United States experience similar forebodings and feelings when they look back at their parenting.

The one answer I heard more than any other, by far, was: "I wish I would have spent more time with my kids." This response accounted for more than a third of all the answers.

Think about this for a second. I asked hundreds of parents the exact same question and tallied my answers. I organized those answers into about fifteen different categories ranging from time spent with kids to discipline style. Out of all of these categories, one category accounted for almost 40 percent of the answers. Parents overwhelmingly look back in regret and wish they would have spent more time just hanging out with their kids.

The testimonials were poignant:

- "I'd fight for each moment with them, no matter how tired I am!"
- "It seems like we were so concerned about placing boundaries that relationship took a far back seat."
- "I would have spent more time making memories, and less time worrying about dishes."
- "More time in conversation, and less time in front of the TV."

- "With a do-over, I'd jump in the ocean with them more instead of sitting on the sand watching them play."

Some of these parents were pretty honest about the excuses they used:

- "It was always easy to say, 'I'm way too tired today!' or 'I have to get this project done, so we'll just do it next week.' And pretty soon we weren't doing those things at all."
- "I think back about the times my kids requested to spend time with me but I was too busy doing what I wanted to do, or quite frankly, sometimes I was 'busy' being lazy or tired."

But the majority of parents also seemed to regret the way they disciplined, particularly in anger:

- "I wish I wouldn't have responded so quickly."
- "A softer voice proved *waaaay* more effective."
- "I learned to postpone my reaction during conflict and dialogue later."

Parents also seemed to regret spending too much time with busy activities like sports:

- "I always liked sports because of the discipline and team building, but sports quickly became a seven-day-a-week commitment that sucked the life out of every other part of her schedule."

- "Sports started as something positive, but soon became the number one priority in all our lives, above family, church, school. . .name it."

The more I asked parents what they'd change, the more I heard the same struggles—struggles I knew all too well.

It's funny, but these vulnerable lessons we all are initially too scared to share with others—these are pure gold to other parents! I know this because occasionally I will share these words: "Here's where I messed up. . . ."

Whenever I say those words during one of my parenting workshops, you can hear a pin drop. Parents are on the edge of their seats.

"And here's what I'd do different next time. . . ."

That's when every pen in the room begins writing furiously. People want to know what works and what doesn't work in the world of parenting.

HINDSIGHT IS 20/20

Effective parenting requires humility and teachability. The fact that you picked up this book reveals you are a learner. I applaud you.

And now I hope to help you in a way that I wish someone would have helped me. I hope to provide you with hindsight I only wish I could have had access to ahead of time.

This kind of knowledge is treasure!

This book holds many truths I have learned the hard way. These truths aren't peculiar or unique to me. In fact, when you read them, you'll probably have seen evidence or the "birth pains" of some of these in your own home already. Maybe you just haven't identified them yet. Some of you might have been practicing some of these habits, good and bad, at least in part already. You've probably noticed their effectiveness. . .or lack thereof.

As I look back at my own parenting and notice key areas where I improved, I compare and fuse those practices with the wisdom and experiences I've gleaned from other parents. I have the unique privilege of mingling with thousands of parents at the parenting workshops I teach each month across the world (and you'd be surprised how similar the struggles are of parents in Kampala, Uganda, and in Lincoln, Nebraska). After these workshops, my wife and I always hang out at the back table and dialogue with parents, listening to stories and trying our best to answer tough questions. It's amazing how often I hear parents share similar mistakes—mistakes I recognize all too well—and wish they could go back and approach their parenting differently.

If only they had a do-over.

Let's face it. Hindsight is 20/20.

Let's not waste time. Let's dive in to the seven vital parenting changes I'd make if I had a do-over.

CHANGE 1

TIP THE SCALES

"My seventeen-year-old daughter won't even talk with me."

The middle-aged mom had wandered into my Get Your Teenager Talking workshop looking for answers. She dabbed at her eyes with a tissue, being careful not to smear her mascara. "I don't know what to do."

"Tell me about your conversations," I asked.

After a little digging, I listened as she recalled her last few conversations with her daughter. I use the word *conversation* loosely. More like *interrogation*.

- "Did you finish your homework?"
- "Did you clean your bathroom?"
- "What time did you get home last night?"
- "Were you with that boy Chris? I knew I shouldn't have let you hang out with that boy!"

As she unveiled what dialogue looked like in her home, the answer quickly became clear. Her daughter didn't want to talk with her mom because in her mind, her mom was acting like a parole officer searching for malfeasance.

Think about it. Would you want to answer this mom's questions? Probably not. You'd be scared your answers would get you in trouble.

That's why most of the dialogue in this home would be more accurately described as *monologue*. Mom talked. Daughter didn't.

As this woman shared her story, I immediately recognized her dilemma because I had made the same mistake with my oldest. My focus on *boundaries* had hindered *bonding*.

BONDING AND BOUNDARIES

At times these two important parenting practices seem almost at odds with each other.

- *Bonding* is playing with your kid, going out for french fries, getting slaughtered by your son in the newest Madden game, laughing and talking together on a comfy couch in the corner of your daughter's favorite coffeehouse.
- *Boundaries* is when we tell our kids it's time for bed, charge their phones on the kitchen counter while they're asleep, or tell them, "No, sorry, you can't stay out that late on Friday. . .especially with that boy Chris!"

Both are essential, and most parents tend to gravitate toward one or the other.

Ask yourself, Which do I lean toward? Which would my kids say I lean toward?

Now ask yourself another question: Which of these two parenting practices do I think most parents look back at later and wish they had done more?

Since you read the opening chapter to this book, you probably can guess the answer. In fact, the number one parenting practice moms and dads shared with me where they experienced the most regret was in the area of bonding.

"I wish I would have spent more time with my kids."

It's the number one area where parents wish they could have a do-over. They wish they had connected with their kids more and just "hung out." In contrast, only a small handful of parents (less than 2 percent polled) said they wished they had applied more boundaries.

Let that sink in for a moment. Most parents enter into this parenting thing favoring either bonding or boundaries. Rarely is someone perfectly balanced. And after most parents finish raising their kids, the vast majority of them wish they would have tipped the scales toward bonding.

I know I wish I would have.

Don't get me wrong. I'm not in any way trying to convince you to let your kids do whatever they want. Not even close. Reread what I've written in the previous pages if you must. Both bonding and boundaries are equally important. What I'm trying to communicate is simply this: Don't skimp on bonding! Most parents look back and feel like they missed out on opportunities to bond and connect with their kids.

As I look back at how I parented my oldest, I definitely put too much weight on boundaries. When I walked into the room, I almost felt it my duty to be a drill sergeant, barking orders.

"Alec, shoes off the couch!"

"Put your glass on a coaster!"

Then I'd use the opportunity to question him, checking up on him.

"Did you finish your homework? Room clean? Trash taken out?"

As Alec grew into his teen years, I noticed something. When I'd walk in the room, he'd get nervous. He'd immediately start thinking, *What am I doing wrong? I'm always doing something wrong.*

Why did he think this?

Because that had become my job. *To correct my kids.*

My motives were pure. I wanted to teach my kids discipline and responsibility. Sadly, I believe my laser focus on boundaries hurt our relationship.

If our kids see us as drill sergeants, bonding will be hindered. Who wants to hang out with the parent who is making their life miserable?

Take this a step further. Who are they going to go to when they mess up or are facing a moral dilemma? Surely they *won't* go to the person who seems ready to pounce on them every time they do wrong.

If I share with Dad, I know he'll freak out!

If I ask Mom about this, she won't help me—she'll just bust me!

Here's where the parenting strategy becomes a little counterintuitive. We think strict boundaries will help teach our kids values. But if we put too much weight on boundaries and neglect bonding, then our kids won't feel safe to open up to us and we'll miss key opportunities to walk through life with them and teach them discernment. In other words, when Mom or Dad doesn't have a relationship with their kids, their kids tend to glean values and behaviors from other sources.

The parent who bonds with their kids has more opportunities to dialogue about real life. The closer the bond, the more they'll absorb.

Bonding opens the doorway to applying boundaries.

So do parents still need to provide boundaries?

Absolutely. Just not like a tyrant. Parents don't need to jump into inspection mode every time they see their kids.

So what does this actually look like day to day? How can we tip the scales toward bonding?

CONNECTION VENUES

The best way to tip the scales is by seeking out settings I like to call *connection venues*. This has become increasingly difficult in a world where people connect with screens more than they connect with human beings. And I'm not just talking about kids. The overwhelming majority of American moms and dads actually spend more time staring at a screen than talking with their spouse or kids. And now that most of us have access to mobile devices, our screen time is increasing, and good ol'-fashioned face-to-face time is decreasing.

What's the result?

Sadly, it's exactly what I shared at the beginning of this book. A huge number of parents are looking back in hindsight and wishing they had devoted more time to simply hanging out with their kids. *"I would have worked less and played with them more!"*

Have you ever spent time with someone lying on his or

her deathbed? Those final moments often bring clarity to what we truly hold dear. Rarely do you see someone asking for their laptop so they can check their work e-mail. The typical request is to be surrounded by family and friends. Sometimes lifelong grudges are forgiven and forgotten in those final moments.

I've never heard someone say, "I wish I would have spent more time at the office!"

I've never heard someone say, "I wish I would have streamed more Netflix!"

People value connection with the people they care about. And we don't need to wait until our deathbed to initiate this kind of connection. We should be searching for any opportunity to connect while our kids are still young and in the home.

Think about the last time you engaged in a meaningful conversation with your kids. Where were you? What initiated that conversation? Is that something you can duplicate and try again?

Note: I didn't ask when you last "exchanged words with your kids." I want you to think about the last time you sat down and truly talked, laughed together, or cried together. What was it about this venue that kindled that kind of conversation?

When I ask parents where this kind of meaningful dialogue occurs in their home, the setting I hear more than any other is the family dinner. In fact, in my survey of what parents would do over, I kept hearing moms and dads say, "More family dinners."

The family dinner is one of those staple connection

points for families. Most people use their hands to eat, so that typically means setting the phone or tablet aside. . .for a few minutes, at least.

Our family even declared family dinners *tech free*. We called it "No Tech at the Table." Funny. . .more conversation happened at our family dinners than in almost any other setting. Think about that for a second. In this particular situation, our *boundary* of "No Tech at the Table" opened the doorway to *bonding* moments. As you can see, boundaries can help create an atmosphere where bonding takes place.

We need to be on the lookout for places where meaningful communication occurs in our homes and be proactive to seek out these venues.

Where are these connection venues in your home?

In a world so full of distractions, parents are beginning to take notice of these venues where their kids almost naturally open up. Another one of these settings is bedtime. An empty-nester parent shared with me:

> *I wish I had cherished bedtime more than I did. I used to pray with my kids and tuck them in when they were young, but the routine eventually faded. However, every once in a while when I'd take the time to tuck them in, it usually resulted in a pleasant conversation. Something about them being tucked neatly in their bedsheets. It's like the sleepiness made them chattier than normal.*

It's interesting to observe which of these connection venues work with your own kids. Different young people will respond to different venues. I became so fascinated by these kinds of settings I wrote an entire book on the subject, *52 Ways to Connect with Your Smartphone Obsessed Kid*, providing dozens of ideas for connecting with today's kids who typically won't pry their eyes from their mobile devices.

Ask yourself: Where do my kids tend to open up more and engage in meaningful conversation? How can I create more of these opportunities in our typical weekly schedule?

I'll be honest with you. Bonding takes time. That's why you shouldn't overthink it. If you see an opportunity. . .

Just Say Yes

Just say yes to any opportunity to bond, no matter how inconvenient. I call this the "yes factor." I tried this with my younger two kids, and the results were revolutionary.

No joke—this morning, as I write this—my eighteen-year-old daughter, Ashley, came up to me and asked, "Dad, do you want to go on a bike ride?"

Allow me to put this into perspective. This is an eighteen-year-old asking her parent to do something together. This isn't a four-year-old. When my kids were four, they asked me to do something with them every ten minutes.

"Daddy, will you play Barbies with me?"

"Daddy, will you watch *Aladdin* with me?"

"Daddy, will you play Velociraptor with me?"

When our kids become teenagers, everything changes. Many parents can count on one hand how many times their teen asked them to hang out in any given month. . .*or year.*

Ashley is pretty social, and we hang out quite a bit. So when she asked me to ride bikes this morning, I hesitated. Not because I didn't want to ride bikes and not because I didn't want to hang out with Ashley, but probably for the same reason many of you would have hesitated. My schedule is jam-packed right now! And when life's to-do list is stacked to the ceiling, "hanging out" seems to get shoved to the back burner.

I easily thought of twenty plausible reasons why I should say no: I've been gone the last three weekends in a row speaking, I have two book deadlines in the next forty-five days, I have two articles due in the next four days, I've got a stack of administrative tasks in my inbox, and work aside, my backyard is a mess, I promised my wife I'd help her shop for a present for my other daughter, Alyssa, today. . . the list goes on. My guess is you have a list that rivals mine.

Every ounce of wisdom in my body was saying, "Jonathan, it's completely reasonable for you to say no. She'll understand."

So I gave her my answer.

"Yes. I'd love to."

So we ventured on a one-hour bike ride on a trail that parallels the American River not twelve minutes from my house. And it was one of the most rewarding times I've had with Ashley in months.

Maybe it's because I actually listened to my own advice from my previous book about connecting with the smartphone generation. One of the ways to connect with today's overconnected kids is seeking out settings where kids naturally break free from their devices to enjoy their immediate surroundings. Bike rides are a no-brainer. It's hard to text while riding a bike.

That's probably why Ashley and I literally talked for an hour without a single interruption (well. . .besides the squirrel I almost hit as it darted across the bike path). We talked about movies, music, college, friendships, conflict, and personality types. We even talked about parenting. It was probably one of the deeper talks we've had in a while.

All because I simply said yes.

I didn't always say yes.

Sadly, this experience with Ashley only happened because I learned the hard way that saying no is a mistake. My parenting repertoire is filled with stories of feeling too busy, too overwhelmed, burning the candle at both ends; you probably know the feeling. It's these times I answer with the most logical response when a person doesn't have any time. Like the time my son Alec asked me if I wanted to play video games with him. I can remember the moment like it was yesterday.

He was in his late teens, working almost every day after school, and had an internship at church. It was an extremely busy time in his life. My schedule was very comparable. I worked full-time writing and speaking, was attending graduate school, volunteered at the church, was raising three kids—not a lot of free time.

Alec poked his head into my office one Friday and simply asked, "Dad, do you wanna play Xbox?"

I was finishing some last-minute prep for a parenting workshop I was teaching that weekend. The next morning I was going to leave the house at 3:30 a.m. on the first flight out. With time in airports, two planes, and a rental car, I'd travel over ten hours across the country (the problem with living in California and frequently speaking on the East Coast) then teach a two-hour workshop Saturday night, preach the morning services at a church Sunday morning, then teach a parenting workshop that afternoon. I had about seven items to finish on my to-do list, and playing video games just didn't seem wise, if even possible.

I can't remember my exact words, but they were something like, "Sorry, Alec, but I've got to finish my workshop helping other moms and dads be good parents."

Yes, the word *irony* comes to mind.

He wasn't brokenhearted. He was actually very kind about it. I can still see the expression on his face. "That's okay, Dad. I understand. I know you'll do a good job."

Fast-forward two days later when in the middle of my parenting workshop I gave the parents a "self-quiz" that helped them look introspectively at how well they knew their kids. As they sat in their seats, pens and pencils busily scratching out answers, I read through the questions myself while standing onstage waiting. As a joke, I played the famous '70s folk song "Cat's in the Cradle," in which a dad expresses his parenting regrets. I jested that they shouldn't feel guilty if they did poorly on the quiz.

That's when it happened.

I began reading my own quiz questions and my eyes rested on question number 13: "When is the last time you played with your kid?"

The lyrics to "Cat's in the Cradle" resounded in my ears: a kid asking his dad to throw a ball and the dad saying, "Not today."

I started full-on weeping.

I turned my back to the audience in hopes they wouldn't notice. I had forty-five seconds to pull it together. But first things first. I whipped my phone out of my pocket and texted my son:

ALEC, I'M A TURD! YOU ASKED ME TO PLAY XBOX WITH YOU AND I LET MY WORK INTERFERE. I'LL TOTALLY PLAY XBOX WITH YOU WHEN I GET HOME TOMORROW! YOU GOT TIME?

Not ten seconds later I got a text back: *SURE. WE'LL BLOW AWAY ZOMBIES!*

The next day I got up bright and early and flew home (another ten-hour journey with a layover), and when my son walked in the door I was sitting on the couch with the controller in my hand. "You ready to show me how to play this thing?"

And we played for almost two hours until he finally had to go to work.

Let me be very clear. Say yes to any opportunity to connect with your teenager.

SINGLE-PARENT/SPLIT HOMES

I have countless friends who are either raising their kids by themselves or shipping kids back and forth to a different parent because of a divorce or separation. These friends always ask me, "Jonathan, how does this work in a split home?"

I have good news for these parents. Everything I say about bonding in this book is 100 percent applicable to kids in split homes. Bonding is potent. The connection between parent and child is powerful. And single parents will want to strive to make these connections just like any other parent. So the first four vital changes we walk through in this book apply to *all parents* regardless of their family's makeup.

The difficult part for split homes is boundaries. One of the chief complaints I hear from moms or dads who have partial custody is that they are teaching one set of values, and then the other half of the week the kids are learning a completely different set of values. Boundaries in each home can differ drastically.

But here's what I think you'll find intriguing. Much of what I talk about in the final three chapters in this book has to do with "walking with" our kids on this journey and teaching them as we go. The boundaries are intrinsically linked with bonding. So even in those chapters parents raising their kids in split homes will find hope in the time they spend with their kids. Your bonding efforts will have more impact than you know.

In my two decades of youth ministry, I spent bonding time with a lot of young people, sometimes only an hour or two per kid per week. It was amazing to see what kind of impact God was able to make even in these short snippets of time. I'm not giving you an excuse to ignore your kids and only give them an hour or two. I say this simply to encourage you not to underestimate the impact of your time connecting with your kids.

So single moms or dads, divorced parents, grandparents. . . *Leave It to Beaver* families—it doesn't matter. Make every effort to seek out these connection venues.

"I Don't Have Time"

I can hear it now. "But Jonathan, I can't just drop everything! I work. I have a life." Or the inevitable. . ."I don't have time."

The lawyer in me is coming out.

Exhibit A: Do you know how much time the average "adult" spends each day soaking in entertainment media and technology?

Add it up on your fingers really quick. Add up all your TV time, computer time, Facebook, smartphone, newspapers and magazines if you actually still read them. . . .

A big part of my job is studying youth culture and technology. So I look at these reports all the time. And I've seen reports that would blow your mind. But let me just share with you a very conservative report when it comes to how many hours adults spend with entertainment media and technology. It's the most recent report from Nielsen, and it reveals that the average adult devotes an average of nine hours and fifty-one minutes per day to entertainment media and technology.[1]

The biggest chunk of time is spent on TV. The average adult spends four hours and fifty-nine minutes daily watching TV, both live and DVR/time-shifted TV.

Now I know many of you might be saying, "I don't watch five hours of TV per day!" Don't worry; if you watch very little TV, then someone on your street, across town, or across the country is watching more than enough TV to make up for you. The average is four hours and fifty-nine minutes. The statistics are even more fascinating when you break them down by age, because teens (ages 12 to 17) average less than three hours a day of TV, while moms and dads (ages 35 to 49) average about four and a half. Then there's Grandpa (age 65 and up)! He watches over seven hours a day! That's a lot of *NCIS*!

My point? And I'll speak directly, as a fellow parent who has struggled with this. Don't tell me you don't have time.

Some of us let our jobs get in the way. We work long hours, and when we're home, we might be physically present, but we're still technically at work on our phone and our laptop. I've heard parents share this struggle for years. "Gotta earn that extra paycheck to pay for football camp and gymnastics."

Guess what your kids need more than football camp and gymnastics?

They need you!

Take it from this single mom I surveyed while researching this book:

> *I wish I could do over the amount of time I spent with my kids, especially as teens. As a single mom, I worked two jobs that kept me very busy during their teen years. One memory in particular was on a Sunday while I was working, my son went to our church and gave his life to Christ. He called me to tell me this, and that he had something else he needed to tell me when I got home. However, the moment passed, and he never discussed it until years later.*

Consider this. I have never—and I mean ever—met an empty nester who told me, "I spent more than enough time with my kids!"

In fact, the typical 20/20 look-back is: "I wish I would have spent a little more time with Michael." "I could have paid more attention to Taylor."

Say yes to any opportunity to connect with your kid.

Does this mean we need to drop everything every time our toddler wants us to play Legos? No. If we said yes to toddlers every time, we'd never get anything done. But by the time your kids are tweens or teens, I'd go out on a limb and say if they want to hang out with you, "Say yes every time." I could even say it another way: "Say yes a minimum of once a day to any opportunity to hang out with your kid." The fact is, 99 percent of teenagers won't ask to hang out more than once a week, much less once a day. So if they do, slide everything aside to make hangout time happen.

I probably didn't realize this until my oldest was already out of the house and I was watching time slip away with my two high school daughters. It was then that I made a pledge to myself: "I don't care how big the pile is on my desk—I'm saying yes to any opportunity to hang out."

These opportunities came in bizarre forms. They weren't always fun and they weren't always things I wanted to do. Sometimes it was my daughter Alyssa coming in and sighing, "Dad, want to go to the DMV with me? I have to renew my license."

"Woo-hoo! The DMV!" (Does the movie *Zootopia* come to mind?)

She wasn't even that excited to hang out with me; she

just didn't want to go to the stinking DMV by herself.

I snagged the opportunity. In fact, I even asked, "Do you wanna grab a Jamba on the way home?" and extended our time together.

You have time. Make time. Even if it turns out to be a drag.

That's the thing about quality time. It takes *quantity* time. We can't choose quality-time moments. They just happen. It takes painfully boring DMV trips, family dinners that sometimes seem like a waste of time and effort, drives to school together, time spent tucking our kid into bed every night—it takes connecting time and time again to achieve those quality-time moments.

If your kids are going through adolescence, then these moments of connection are even more vital. Not just because our interactions with them are fewer and farther between, but because research actually reveals that quantity time pays off with adolescents more than with any other age.

I'm referring to a fascinating new study out of the *Journal of Marriage and Family* that argues mere quantity time is *not* enough. Yes, you read that correctly. It doesn't pay off just to clock in hours hanging out with our kids. Don't be confused. Hear me out.

This study compared the time parents spent with kids of different ages and revealed a surprising difference between young kids and adolescents. The amount of time parents spend with their kids between the ages of three and eleven has virtually no correlation to how children turn out. What's more, the study found "one key instance when parent time can be particularly harmful to children. That's when parents, mothers in particular, are stressed, sleep-deprived, guilty and anxious."[2]

Hold the phone! Does this mean we shouldn't "hang" with our kids?

Keep reading.

Notice this finding related to kids between ages three and eleven. If we keep reading the report, the authors note one key instance when quantity time *does* matter.

Adolescence.

And I quote:

> *The more time a teen spends engaged with their mother, the fewer instances of delinquent behavior. And the more time teens spend with both their parents together in family time, such as during meals, the less likely they are to abuse drugs and alcohol and engage in other risky or illegal behavior. They also achieve higher math scores.*[3]

This new report isn't alone in these findings. Columbia University has been noting the link between "quantity time" and raising healthy teens for years in its Family Dinners reports.[4] These discoveries are particularly intriguing considering this is the time when many stay-at-home moms feel unneeded and consider jumping back into the workforce.

So what can we take away from this new report? After all, it seems to contradict conventional wisdom that the more time moms and dads spend with young kids, the better.

I think this report brings to light several realities I've witnessed firsthand:

1. *Mere proximity doesn't produce quality time.* If we bring our kids to the grocery store with us, ignoring them the entire time, talking on our phones, occasionally barking at them, "Put that down!". . .we aren't clocking healthy bonding time. Bonding necessitates dialogue. So if you're going to drag your kids on errands with you, make it fun. Interact with them. Ask them their favorite meal and have them help you shop for it. Do more listening than talking. Make them feel noticed and heard. (We'll explore how to do all this later in the book.)

2. *Adolescents have different needs than younger kids.* Just when our teens—and even tweens—begin pushing us away, they need us the most. No, that doesn't mean we need to smother them or put them on a leash. It simply means parents need to be especially proactive about looking for opportunities to bond with their teens. Healthy parenting requires healthy investments of both bonding and boundaries. Are you investing in both? Which bank is getting more deposits this month?

3. *Don't use quality time as an excuse to avoid quantity time.* If your kids are like mine, you'll experience just one or two quality-time moments for every dozen times you hang out with your kids. Quality time usually necessitates quantity time. Parents need to clock quantity hours having fun with their kids, talking, laughing. . .*listening*! You never know when quality-time moments will materialize.

Spending time with our kids creates an interesting dynamic. On one hand, we really need to be proactive about doing it, because our tendency as humans is to get caught up in our own world. On the other hand, spending time with our kids should never be just a check mark in a box. *I clocked in three hours today.* In fact, our time investment should be without expectation of what that time will look like, not just seeking the "quality" but really showing our kids that they are *worthy* of our time. Period.

What can you do this week to truly connect with your child?

THE BOUNDARY FAST

Some of you might be reading this chapter and thinking, *I'm that guy he described at the beginning of the chapter. I'm the drill sergeant. My dialogue with my kids typically involves checking up on them or disciplining them.*

What can we do to tip the scales if the scales are already tilted completely the opposite way?

All parents need to be proactive about practicing bonding. But if your scales are already weighted completely toward boundaries, you're going to need to work extra hard to reverse this trend. You may even need to go on a *boundary fast.* This means walking in a room and completely stifling the urge to ask your kids if they've finished their homework and chores. . .and just playing with them instead. Try it.

Again, I'm not saying that boundaries aren't good. I'm talking to the person who is so focused on boundaries, they rarely bond with their kids. If that's you, then try going twenty-four hours without giving any instruction to your kids at all. If the damage is really bad, you may need to go an entire week. For that week, don't allow yourself to discipline, correct, or advise in any way. Instead, look for opportunities to bond.

Maybe you aren't a tyrant and you don't need a boundary fast. Maybe you are just like the majority of parents who feel like bonding is important, and you want to make sure you maximize these opportunities while you can. So look for these moments. Seek out settings where connection happens. Say yes to every opportunity to connect; and if your kids never ask you to connect, that's all the more reason to be seeking out communication settings. Take the initiative. Give your children a taste of your full attention.

What are some of the ways we can tip the scales toward bonding?

LIVING IT OUT THIS WEEK

QUESTIONS TO DISCUSS WITH YOUR SPOUSE AND/OR OTHER PARENTS

1. When parents look back in hindsight, why do you think far more of them regret missing opportunities to bond rather than placing too few boundaries?
2. *Bonding* or *boundaries*: Which way is your scale tipped? What does that look like in your home?
3. Which way would your kids say your scale is tipped? Why?
4. What are some connection venues that have worked with your kids?
5. What is it about those settings that seems to kindle conversation? Can you duplicate those factors in other settings? How?
6. What are some specific connection venues you think might be worth trying with your kids?
7. Do you think a boundary fast might be an experiment worth trying in your home? What do you think will happen?
8. What is one thing you read in this chapter that you would like to implement this week? When will you try it?

CHANGE 2

LET IT GO

One of my daughters walked into the kitchen to find something to eat.

"I bought some of those rolls you like for your sandwiches," I offered.

"Why would I want a sugary roll for my sandwich?" she said, and grabbed a loaf of bread instead.

This is how many conversations can begin with teenagers. They aren't defiant; they probably couldn't even be classified as back-talking. They're just. . .*argumentative.*

If you have teenagers, you've experienced it firsthand.

"The sky sure is a pretty blue today."

"Actually, it's more of a purple."

Sigh.

That's what it felt like in the kitchen that day with my daughter.

"My bad," I said. "The other day you told me you were sick of plain ol' bread. These are those really good Hawaiian rolls."

She picked up the rolls, inspected them with disdain, then dropped them back on the counter. "These are too many calories."

Okay, it was decision time: Let it go, or jump into lawyer mode and show evidence to the contrary?

I mistakenly opted for lawyer mode.

"Actually, those are lower calories than two pieces of the bread you just pulled out. And they taste better." I smiled, proud of myself.

She looked at the rolls again. "Yeah, but these are too small. Why would I want a sandwich that small?" She smirked condescendingly.

Now I was mad!

Just yesterday she told me she didn't want such large portions; now the rolls were "too small." She didn't even make sense. She was being inconsistent. She was arguing. . .*just to argue*.

And that's when I realized I needed to just shut up and let it go.

She was *not* arguing that she didn't want my bread. What she wanted was *independence*. She wanted to choose her food without anyone telling her what she should eat. My suggestion of rolls was received as, "You should eat a sandwich." Her retorts were saying, "I'll eat whatever I want. I'm a big girl. Leave me alone."

It's hard raising adolescents. Their natural instinct is to vie for independence.

Bonnie Maslin, PhD, author of *Picking Your Battles*, says, "It helps to view the push-back as less about defying you and more about saying 'I gotta be me!' "[1]

Think about this for a moment. Our kids want to be able to make decisions on their own. This is *not* a negative characteristic. It is positive in every way. We should want this. We should celebrate this!

Funny, in their later teen years I've given my girls plenty

of independence. But sometimes even "sandwich selections" could be received as micromanagement. My daughter's snippety little banter wasn't an all-out rebellion; it was a reminder to give her space.

And to think. . .I almost turned sandwich selection into a major battle.

Don't Sweat the Small Stuff

"If you could give just one piece of advice to the parents in this audience, what would it be?"

That was the question I posed to the panel of parents gathered on the stage of this particular parenting class. This was the final session in a parenting series I taught, and instead of wrapping it up with another keynote from me, I brought four sets of grandparents onstage, empty nesters whose kids were all grown up with kids of their own. The pastor of the church recommended these four couples.

"They're not only solid believers; they're very real. They'll be happy to share both their successes and their failures," he'd said.

And that's what they did. I asked them about their worst mistakes as parents, the guidelines that worked, and the ones that didn't work so well. The wealth of wisdom and experience flowing from the stage that day was priceless.

I closed with the question about the "one piece of advice" they'd give to parents in the audience.

All four couples shared. I don't even remember three of the answers, but I'll never forget what a guy named Marshall shared. He said: "Don't sweat the small stuff."

He went on to tell a story about trying to teach his

daughter a lesson and finally realizing, "The very act of correcting was becoming so tedious and problematic that it was creating a worse problem than the original infraction."

As he shared the story, I couldn't help but think, *Been there!* I identified with his description more than he would ever know. Let that sink in for a moment:

"The very act of correcting was becoming so tedious and problematic that it was creating a worse problem than the original infraction."

Bingo!

I had committed this mistake countless times.

"Did you floss your teeth?"

"No."

"What? Do you realize how much we have spent on braces, and you're just throwing that away? Sit down and let me share with you thirty-seven reasons you need to floss regularly. . . ."

I needed someone to slap me and say, "Jonathan. Let it go! What's more important—your kid flossing, or your relationship with your kid?"

I'm not alone in this struggle. My good friend Gary recently asked me, "Jonathan, I've told my daughter thirteen times to put away her towels after she showers. We found almost a dozen towels in the corner of her room yesterday because she never puts them away. What should we do?"

As I heard this question, I couldn't help but put it in perspective. We had one of our kids really rebel growing up. So the first question I asked my friend was, "Is she sneaking out of the house?"

"No."

"Flunking algebra?"

"No. No. She's getting over a 4.0."

"Is she smoking pot in her room?"

He laughed and said, "No."

I smiled. "Then tell her since she likes to collect towels, it's time for her to do her own laundry. Tell her once, hand her a box of detergent. . .*and then let it go*."

Five years ago I would *not* have known to give that advice. But now that I've seen my kids go off to school and begin making choices on their own, I have grown increasingly confident I should have "let it go" more often and given them all even more opportunities to learn lessons on their own.

Don't misunderstand. I'm not saying, "Allow your kids to disobey and talk smack."

If you tell your kid to put their towel away and they ignore you, then warn them, and if they keep doing it, apply a natural consequence whereby they can learn that lesson themselves.

Ask yourself, What could be a good natural consequence of hoarding bath towels? Maybe have them do their own laundry. They're going to have to do laundry when they move out, right? Might as well give them some practice now since they seem to be vying for that independence.

Don't ground them for a week because they don't hang up towels.

In the same way, if your kids are rude, feel free to tell them, "Hey, you don't need to talk smack when I tell you to put your towels away." Or, "I don't mind if you want to make your own lunch. But don't be rude to me. I was trying to be nice and buy you the bread you liked." (Then refrain from adding their favorite adage—"Just sayin'!")

Correct their rudeness. . .*and then let it go*. They'll respect you more for not dwelling on it. Don't turn every mistake into an opportunity to correct, lecture, or rebuke, to the point where *your very act of correcting becomes so tedious and problematic that it creates a worse problem than the original infraction* (Marshall's definition again).

One of the parents I surveyed said it like this: "I would use the strategy of 'turn and walk away' in conflict situations instead of letting myself get sucked up into the crazy."

I love that. "Sucked up into the crazy."

Raising kids isn't easy. Raising young men and women is even harder. But try to remember how hard it was being that age. Today's teenagers are currently the most stressed age group. They're balancing a huge load, they're worried about the future. . .and they're dealing with all this stress with raging hormones and a brain that isn't fully developed. Don't allow yourself to get caught up in the crazy.

Let it go!

Don't sweat the small stuff.

Be happy when they want to make their own decisions, and be there for them when they need your help. In just a few years, they'll be making all their decisions on their own.

Are you preparing them for that day?

Easier Said Than Done

If you're like me, you're probably thinking, *Jonathan, this sounds really good on paper, but the fact is, when I get in the moment, I can't think this fast!*

I completely understand. I can't tell you how many situations I reflected on later and came up with some great ideas of responses I *should have made*. . .but didn't in the moment.

So what does letting it go truly look like? How do we pave the pathway toward picking our battles?

Let's take a look at four steps.

FOUR STEPS TO ACTUALLY LETTING IT GO
Step 1: Spot It

The first step to letting it go is being able to spot the moment when you actually need to let it go. Sometimes these moments sneak up on you. I know they snuck up on me all the time.

I remember a particular December morning back when my younger daughter, Ashley, was a freshman in high school. She came walking down the stairs from her bedroom as we headed to the car.

And that's when I said it—the words that would start the fight of the year. I asked her, "Where is your coat?"

Her reply was simple. "I don't need a coat!"

That's how the argument started. Sounds innocent enough, right? It's 28 degrees outside. Isn't it logical for a dad to ask his fourteen-year-old daughter where her coat is?

That's what I thought. Fast-forward just two minutes and you would have witnessed a full-blown apocalypse— tears, yelling, a backpack getting airborne. Even the dog retreated to the other room.

Where was that sweet little girl who used to look up to me with her big green eyes and call me "Daddy"?

Apparently I didn't get the memo that there was a jacket shortage in the house.

Strike that!

Thirteen different girls' jackets inhabited our front closet, just no *fashionable* jackets worthy of a stylish freshman girl. That's why my coat mandate was met with such opposition.

I didn't see it coming. Having no clue this spat would forever be remembered in the McKee house as "the coat incident of 2012," I maintained my ground.

"Sorry, Ashley, it's December. The cars are covered with ice. You can see your breath. The cat is frozen solid on the back lawn! Put on a jacket and get in the car!"

Houston, we have liftoff.

She flipped out.

No need to tell you the rest of that story. If you have a teenage daughter, you've *lived* that story.

What was I missing here? Was I that clueless? Does raising teenage girls require *drama*? Was this an MTV reality show or my house?

Here was the problem. To me, wearing any old jacket wasn't a big deal. To her, it was a huge deal. This difference in opinion made the situation difficult.

These kinds of situations sideswipe parents frequently. We don't see them coming. Next thing we know, our kids are enraged because of something we said or did. We didn't realize wearing a coat was such a big deal. That's why parents need to be on guard for these moments and be ready to identify them before they escalate.

What does this look like in your home?

Picture a time when an argument grew heated in your home, one that, come to think of it, was completely avoidable. If you had a do-over, could you go back and tweak your response to avoid it?

We need to recognize these arguments when they first sneak up on us. We need to tell ourselves, "Even though I don't think this is a big deal, my daughter actually does think this is a big deal."

My wife is way better at spotting these situations with my daughters than I am. That's probably because I have that mutant male gene. I don't understand all the emotions behind half of these decisions.

"What do you mean you have to stop by Target to buy mascara before school? No way! You should have thought of that yesterday." (True story.)

For me, no mascara is no big deal. For my daughter— *major crisis*!

Here's where pride can kick in. Some of us think, *I've got this*. We see an argument coming and we still proceed thinking we can handle it. I can't tell you how many times I've thought, *I've got this*. . .and I didn't have it.

The second we see the fight coming, we need to catch it.

We need to learn to spot these moments so we can move effectively to the next step.

Step 2: Press Pause

This is probably the most important step to prevent ugly conflicts in your home: *Press pause!*

Notice I didn't say give it up. I just said put a pin in it and wait until you're better equipped to deal with it later.

When I'm sideswiped, my tendency is to get up and sideswipe back. I'm actually quite gifted at it. This isn't a skill I should put on my résumé: *able to make people feel incredibly stupid when they step out of line.* That's why it's so important for me to press pause once I recognize a potential conflict brewing. Pausing, or postponing, gives me the time I need to gather my thoughts and put the situation in perspective. Often this moment of clarity reveals that I should just let it go. This isn't always the case, but most often the situation definitely requires less anger and emotion. Pressing pause helps me bring my A-game to the situation.

Most people make way better decisions after they have time to think it over.

But what if you need to make a decision on the fly? Consider the example of my daughter and the coat. When your kid is getting ready to walk out the door for school, it's pretty difficult to say, "Everyone stop right where they are. We need to think about this for ten minutes!"

No way. Ten minutes will make everybody late.

Here's where you have to make a quick decision to let it go—at least until later when you've had more time to think about it. So if you're stuck having to make a speedy decision, ask yourself these questions:

1. By waiting, are you allowing your child to commit a blatant moral blunder?
2. Are you putting her or anyone else in danger?
3. Is it possible that, by waiting, she could actually learn this lesson on her own?

If you answer no to the first two but yes to the third, then by all means, wait!

Who cares if your daughter gets cold. She'll probably remember a jacket next time. What would you rather have: a good relationship with your cold daughter, or a warm daughter who despises you?

It's just a coat. Let it go. (Notice I'm talking to myself here.)

Pressing pause is such an important principle I've devoted an entire chapter to it ("Change 4: Press Pause"), focusing on stopping anger before it grows out of control. So no need to go into great detail here. Read that chapter for some effective principles that helped me avoid destructive angry outbursts with my family.

Pressing pause gives us time to do the next important step.

Step 3: Step into Their Shoes

I wish someone could put an accurate number to what percent of fights are caused by miscommunication.

In my house, that number would have to be in the 90-something range. Why? Because whenever my wife, Lori, and I are done squabbling over something, we always end up saying, "Well, I thought you were saying. . ." or "I thought you meant. . ."

Frequently, we never invested the time to step into their shoes and try to understand the other person's point of view.

In Stephen Covey's popular book *The Seven Habits of Highly Effective People*, he proposes that we "seek first to understand, then to be understood."[2] Covey is paraphrasing Francis of Assisi's famous prayer: "O Divine Master, grant that I may not so much seek to be consoled as to console; to be understood as to understand; to be loved as to love. . . ."[3]

Seek first to understand.

Imagine how many arguments could be avoided if we applied that principle alone!

Step into their shoes. Why are they acting this way?

My kids almost always have a reason for acting the way they do. Sometimes they don't even know the reason, but they have one.

I've seen kids act out just to get the attention of their parents who were ignoring them. You've probably seen this, too. Just look around a restaurant on any given day and spot that dad or mom who is glued to their phone. Sometimes their kids' antics are just their way of screaming, "Mom, notice me." (Something we're going to examine in detail in the next chapter.)

Be sure you're taking the time to pause and truly listen to your kids. Hear their side of the story. Don't be thinking of your arguments as they talk; instead, be considering each of their arguments. In fact, as you listen to them, pretend you are their defense attorney. Listen to every word they say carefully and start preparing their defense in your mind. Make sure you clearly understand where they're coming from. This will help you get to the heart of the situation— and not just dole out some surface punishment.

Our family was close to a teenager named Nicole who got in big trouble with her mom for coming home thirty minutes late one night.

Imagine what you'd do as a parent in this situation. Your seventeen-year-old daughter comes home thirty minutes late, with no phone call. . .*nothing*! Causing you to stay up and worry.

This mom was furious. When Nicole walked in the door, her mom laid into her.

"Do you know how late you are? Do you know how worried I've been? I've been texting you and calling. For all I knew you were on the side of the road dead somewhere!" (Sound familiar?)

Nicole didn't say a word. She just apologized and walked upstairs, crying.

Flustered, the mom went to bed. But something wasn't right. Nicole was never late. And her response was too. . .*evasive*. Why didn't she argue?

This mom got up and went upstairs to find Nicole fully dressed, sobbing on her bed.

The mom sat on the bed by her side and tried to comfort her. "What happened?"

Nicole cried for another minute before saying anything. Finally she managed one sentence. "Tyler broke up with me."

Tyler was her boyfriend of almost two years. He was supposed to take her to a formal dance the next week. This was one of the most devastating evenings of her life, and frankly, being late hadn't even crossed her mind.

Are all our kids' mess-ups because of reasons this dire? Not at all.

But how will we know unless we pause long enough to listen and step into their shoes?

Always ask yourself why they are reacting the way they are:

- Are they tired?
- Are they hungry?

- Are they stressed?
- Did something bad happen at school today?
- Are they being picked on?
- Did they have a bad breakup?
- Could it be something you did?
- Did you and your spouse have a fight last night, which they overheard, and they're worried you'll get a divorce?

Be quick to listen, slow to speak, and slow to get angry (I stole that from the Bible—James 1:19). Seek to understand the why behind their reaction.

This is why *Step 2, press pause,* is so important. Pressing pause buys us the time to do *Step 3, step into their shoes* and try to understand the context of the situation. It gives us the framework to make a good decision.

When my daughter wanted to leave the house without a coat, it should have taken me just three seconds to ask myself if the situation required action right then and there. It didn't. This would have given me all day to think about the situation and consider Ashley's point of view. If I would have just asked her a few questions (which I eventually did) and truly stepped into her shoes, I might have realized that Ashley had been receiving hand-me-down jackets for her entire life. That meant she was always a minimum of two years out of date. I had bought a new jacket for myself that year. How fair was it not to buy one for her?

Sure, some people might find that attitude materialistic. But think about this. She wasn't asking for a new coat. She was just choosing to live without one. Even if I disagreed with her logic, *this was the way she felt*.

Parents always need to step into their kids' shoes and make sure they understand the situation so they can respond wisely.

Only then are we ready for the final step.

Step 4: Pick Your Battles

As I look back at some of the angry outbursts I've had with my kids over the years, I realize many of them were over small issues like wearing jackets, brushing teeth, picking up dirty laundry. . .small stuff I really should have let go at the moment. After walking away from the situation, I often decided the issue wasn't even worth addressing, and for sure wasn't worth freaking out about.

But sometimes the issue does need to be addressed. We shouldn't ignore our kids' bad behaviors. But even then we need to let it go. . .*at first*.

Allow me to explain.

We need to pick our battles. After you (1) spot a potential battle on the horizon, (2) press pause, and (3) step into your kid's shoes, only then can you determine whether it's a battle worth fighting. Ask yourself, is this issue worth addressing? What is it about? Is she violating our core values? Is she in danger? Is this a lesson she needs to be taught? Can she learn it herself?

For example, if your child directly disobeys, then you should do something about it. Just follow the steps above first.

Let's say you tell your seventh-grade son Chris to put his laundry away. He doesn't. And you don't notice this until you're walking out the door with him.

Practice what you've learned in the pages prior:

1. Spot it. If this is one of those moments that could turn into an ugly battle. . .
2. Press pause. Think about your response. Ask yourself, Is this something I should let go? If not, let it go *for now*. First you need to. . .
3. Step into his shoes. Why isn't he putting his clothes away? Is Chris disobedient, lazy, or just truly forgetful? *Hmm. He does miss assignments all the time at school. Maybe remembering is very hard for him.* But does that give him a get-out-of-jail-free card for life's responsibilities? Maybe a warning would be good. If he doesn't listen to that, a natural consequence may help him with these kinds of situations.

Going through those steps helped you decide Chris probably isn't being disobedient; he's just being irresponsible. You don't want to punish him, but you'd like to teach him responsibility.

Sometimes letting it go isn't an option. Sometimes you have to. . .

ADDRESS THE ISSUE

Picking your battles means occasionally you do have to address disagreements or bad behaviors. Our kids may not like it, but that's okay. Life is full of disagreements. And frankly, if we don't teach our kids how to deal with conflict in a healthy way, they'll never learn how to get along with their college roommate, their boss, or their spouse someday.

These discussions require effort and forethought. Some of these exchanges might even feel tedious. That's why it's so essential that you postpone your immediate response, think over the situation, and do everything possible to understand your child's side of the story. Only then do you take up the issue with your child. Don't get heated in this exchange; don't get sucked into the crazy. Just engage in a healthy dialogue, and then let it go.

As for the Chris example, you might say, "Chris, I do your laundry for you because I love you. I'm not your maid. If you can't respect me enough to put your shirts in the drawer after I wash them, dry them, and fold them, then you're going to do your own laundry."

Then let it go.

And if Chris forgets to put away his clothes again, teach him how to do his own laundry. After washing, drying, and folding darks and whites one time, my guess is you won't have to tell him again. If the irresponsibility persists, then he can do his own laundry.

I don't intend to convey that this process is easy. I know for me, it's *never* as easy as it appears in a parenting book!

Here's where good parenting requires lots of energy. Because realistically you'll have to show your kid how to do the laundry when you're trying to teach them that lesson. Then if they neglect their responsibilities again, you'll have to either make them do their own laundry again or just let them wear smelly clothes!

Just remember, natural consequences teach our kids far more than our lectures.

Don't think you're a bad parent if you decide to let it go.

It's even okay to make exceptions.

"Normally I'd make you do your own laundry. But I realize you had a very trying day. Please don't forget next time."

It's okay to let it go.

This process of letting it go and picking your battles will avoid countless conflicts.

I wish I would have used this methodology more often.

LIVING IT OUT THIS WEEK

QUESTIONS TO DISCUSS WITH YOUR SPOUSE AND/OR OTHER PARENTS

1. What is one thing in this chapter that resonated with you?
2. Name a time when you found "the very act of correcting was becoming so tedious and problematic that it was creating a worse problem than the original infraction."
3. Have you seen any evidence of your kids vying for independence? What did you observe?
4. How can you respond when they do this?
5. Which step is the most difficult: spotting the moment when you need to let it go, pressing pause, stepping into your kids' shoes, or picking your battles? Explain.
6. Why is pressing pause so important?
7. Why is stepping into your kids' shoes so important?
8. Give an example of a battle worth fighting.
9. How can you fight this battle. . .without fighting?
10. What is one thing you read in this chapter that you would like to implement this week? When will you try it?

CHANGE 3

NOTICE

When I was in fifth and sixth grade, I began hanging out with some kids at school who were bad influences on me. It's kind of scary to think about bad influences as early as fifth grade, but these guys were definitely bad news. They were completely disrespectful to authority, they talked foul, and the way they talked about their female classmates was providing me with quite an education about anatomy and reproduction.

At first I remember being shocked by what I heard. But after sitting next to one of these guys in class for eight hours a day, I quickly grew numb to his conversation. It became the norm.

By sixth grade I became close friends with several of these guys. They were on my soccer team and we'd hang out together most days of the week.

At this time in my life I was pretty committed to God and my church. My relationship with God was important to me. But in my own sixth-grade world, I was soaking in a lot more input from my friends than from God. God got about one or two hours a week. These friends got about five to ten hours a day.

I won't bore you with the details. Let me just say, my actions started changing. My attitude changed, my vocabulary changed, my whole worldview changed. My parents didn't really notice because I kept these changes under the radar.

It all came to an apex one weekday at soccer practice.

The coach was alone this particular day—no assistant coach. So while Coach was on the other end of the field working with the offense, my friends on the defense were laughing and joking with me and doing drills—much more of the former than the latter. I don't remember the jokes my friends were telling, I don't remember who said what—all I can remember was Coach was all the way on the other side of the field, so we were saying whatever we wanted because no one could hear us.

One of my friends took a shot at the goal and missed. I began running after it. Even though I can't remember my exact words, I remember looking back at my friends laughing and allowing certain words to roll off my tongue. . .words you never would have heard me speak a year prior.

But something was wrong.

My friends were all staring at me in shock.

I couldn't figure it out, because we talked like that all the time. In fact, most of them talked worse. But still they stared, eyes wide open.

I turned away from my friends to look for the ball, and in that very moment their expressions made sense. My dad was standing right there, not ten feet in front of me. He had come out to watch me practice, and by his face, I could tell he had caught it all.

I'll never forget the expression on his face.

It wasn't the *You're in huge trouble when you get home!*

expression I knew so well. (I excelled in mischief as a kid!) His expression was different. It simply conveyed, *Oh. . .so that's who you really are.*

What I saw on my dad's face was realization. At that moment the cat was out of the bag. My dad realized who his boy Jonathan truly had become.

Let's just say it was a quiet car ride home.

That moment was eye-opening for my dad. He began paying more attention to the friends I was hanging out with and the influences I was gleaning from. The more aware he was, the more he was able to make informed parenting decisions. All this began with his simple decision to come watch me at soccer practice one day.

Where would you have to show up to get a glimpse into your kids' world?

Do you know your kids?

- Who do they enjoy hanging out with?
- Who do they spend the most time with?
- What do they talk about?
- Who do they connect with on their devices?
- Have they met all of these people in person?
- Do you know what kinds of pictures they've snapped to one another?
- What do your kids watch for entertainment?
- Would they let you watch it with them?
- What music do they listen to when you're around?
- What about when you're not around?
- What makes them happy?
- What makes them sad?

- Do they feel accepted by others?
- What do they do when they're feeling sad or alone?
- What is their room like?
- What do they do when they're alone in their room?

Do you really know your kids?

Please don't get me wrong. I'm not trying to suggest your kids all deal drugs or watch highly inappropriate Seth Rogan movies (although the latter is quite possible). What I'm really asking is, are you present in their lives enough to get a glimpse of who they really are?

I ask this question simply because many of today's parents are so busy that they become too wrapped up in their own lives to notice what is going on in the bedroom twenty feet down the hall from their own.

I definitely fell into this trap at times. I was busy, my kids were busy, we saw one another at dinner and engaged in a bit of dialogue. Everything must have been fine, right?

Honestly, I wouldn't have known if it wasn't, because I wasn't taking the time or energy to truly notice.

If I had a chance to do it all over again, this is one of the vital changes I'd make. I'd take the time to *notice*.

Under the Radar

What happens when we don't notice?

Sadly, today's young people are really good at slipping under the radar if we let them. Time passes and we think no news is good news. But eventually we receive a wake-up call: a bad report card, a phone call from school or another parent, or maybe even an encounter with law enforcement—something that alerts us that things aren't exactly what they seem.

Have you ever had a surprise like this?

Have you ever looked back and thought, *How did I miss this?*

Last year Diane Sawyer asked Sue Klebold that question. Sue is the mother of Dylan Klebold, one of the Columbine killers. Like many of you, I remember exactly where I was on April 20, 1999, when the news began showing live coverage of students fleeing Columbine High School as two "armed gunmen wearing black trench coats" went on a shooting spree, eventually killing twelve students and one teacher and wounding twenty-four others before turning the guns on themselves.

For years to follow, as Sue Klebold was alternating between living in mourning and in hiding, she would turn on the radio and hear other parents ranting about her: "How could she not have known? She should have noticed something was wrong with her son."

"Before Columbine happened, I would have been one of those parents," Klebold told Diane Sawyer, breaking a sixteen-year silence in a special edition of *20/20*.[1] "I think we like to believe that our love and our understanding is protective, and that 'if anything were wrong with my kids, I would know,' but I didn't know, and I wasn't able to stop him from hurting other people. I wasn't able to stop his hurting himself and it's very hard to live with that."

Sue Klebold didn't see the signs. Two years before the attack, Sue wrote in her diary: *Things have been really happy this summer. . . . Dylan is yukking it up and having a great time with friends.*

Dylan was writing in his own journal at the same time, his words only to be discovered after the shooting: *"Thinking of Suicide. I hate my life. I want to die. I have a nice family, good house, couple of good friends. No girls. Nobody accepting me even though I want to be accepted."*

Sue Klebold didn't notice the signs.

Sawyer asked Klebold point-blank: "Could you have prevented what happened at Columbine?"

With tears in her eyes, the now sixty-six-year-old mom paused and thought hard about the answer. Dabbing her eyes with a tissue, she responded, "If I had recognized that Dylan was experiencing some real mental distress, he would not have been there. He would have gotten help."

If I had recognized. . .

Hindsight is always 20/20.

Very few of us can relate to what this mom experienced, but many of us have been surprised by our kids' behaviors at one time or another. I know I have. And immediately I began thinking, *If only I would have. . .*

If you've missed something, you're not alone. Don't beat yourself up for the past. The important principle is, you can do something about it in the future.

You can *notice*.

No, I'm *not* going to advise you to place a nanny cam in their bedrooms or buy the newest "stalking" software for their phones. I'm going to recommend something far more effective.

Try something in the next twenty-four hours. Put down your phone, turn off the TV, clear away any work, bills, or mail off the counter. . .and just take a moment to notice your kids. Don't spy or offer critique. Just watch them with the intent of getting to know something about them to better understand who they are. Maybe even catch them doing something right or praiseworthy and affirm them.

My wife, Lori, is so good at this with all our kids. Even now, as they are in college, she'll see my oldest daughter post one of her art projects on Instagram, and Lori will text her, *WOW! YOU ARE SO TALENTED! I LOVED THE SKETCH YOU POSTED TODAY!* Lori is shrewd enough not to comment on every post—some young people see this as stalking behavior. It's embarrassing when Mom is always commenting. So Lori will text her affirmations personally. Not every time, but frequently.

Notice them! Even little things: "Thanks for taking the garbage cans in. You're showing a lot of responsibility. Greater responsibility deserves greater freedom." Or "Your eye makeup looks really good. Is that a new eyeliner?"

You can't compliment if you don't notice.

Here's the intriguing part: today's young people yearn to be noticed! And if Mom and Dad don't, others will gladly fill that void.

NOTICE ME!

Last year I was being interviewed about today's youth culture on a popular radio show on the East Coast, and the host asked me an interesting question: "What is the one thing young people want more than anything else today?"

This question made me think. I mean, I could have answered it on so many different levels. If we were talking about material possessions, then the answer would be simple: a smartphone. Young people want a smartphone more than they want a car today. And if they want a car, the most important feature of said car is how it connects with their smartphone.

But is a smartphone all they are truly seeking in life? Or is there something a little more purposeful?

I think the number one cry of young people today is simply this: *"Notice me!"*

Young people want to be liked. They want to be noticed and heard. The world of smartphones and social media has only amplified this yearning.

Last month I read an eye-opening article in the *Washington Post* about what it looks like to be a thirteen-year-old today in the world of likes and longing.[2] The article was spot-on. It described this young girl's iPhone as "the place where all her friends are hanging out." And what were all these friends seeking? Likes and comments. "Over 100 likes is good, for me," the girl said.

Here's where the article got interesting. The girl had 604 Instagram followers but only 25 posts. Why? Because if she doesn't get enough likes, she deletes the pic.

She doesn't want to appear "unliked."

Another article posted the same month from *Tech Insider* interviewed a fifteen-year-old freshman who averaged two to three posts per week on Instagram.[3] If you look at his profile, though, he has only fifteen posts total. Do the math. If a kid has been posting even just two pictures a week, that's over one hundred posts per year. So in the last two years this kid has posted over two hundred pics. . .and kept just fifteen.

Why?

Because they are the ones with the most likes.

Can't have pics without likes.

"Usually if someone has over 500 followers and posts a picture, they expect it to bring in at least 60 likes," he told *Insider*. "Anything less usually means the picture will be deleted."

Today's young people want to be noticed, liked, or a simple *tbh*.

Tbh is a comment you can receive meaning "to be honest" or "to be heard." It verifies what you posted. It's someone agreeing, "What you just posted is true."

It's a simple "I notice you. And what you're saying is valid."

Do you make your kids feel that way?

Notice, I didn't ask you if you "liked" one of their pictures or commented "tbh" on one of their posts. There's a fine line between noticing our kids and *stalking* our kids!

It's a delicate balance. Our kids want to be noticed. . .but they don't want Mom or Dad watching their every move!

Our kids desperately want someone to notice them, like them, value them. They want this acceptance from friends, from romantic interests, and even from Mom and Dad!

As they grow to be tweens and teens, their acknowledgment of the latter will start to diminish. They would love Mom and Dad's emotional support but would prefer to avoid their meddling. This is to be expected from young adults who are slowly beginning to make more decisions for themselves. Many of them are striving for independence. Don't mistake that as a desire to be ignored. Kids want their parents' love and affirmation.

Author and social researcher Shaunti Feldhahn found this to be remarkably evident in her research. She surveyed about three thousand teens asking them questions about their parents' involvement in their lives and discovered "almost all (94 percent) said that if they could wave a magic wand, the perfect situation would be one in which their parents actively worked to be involved with them." Feldhahn pleads with parents, "No matter how aloof your teens seem to be, force yourself to remember that they *want* you to be part of their lives—and do the work to get there."[4]

Just take note of any kid who has been ignored by Mom or Dad, and you'll see this desire to be noticed by Mom and Dad is markedly apparent. I've seen countless examples in my years working with teenagers. Take "Stephanie," for example.

I met Stephanie when she was in middle school. She was one of about fifty tweens I interacted with weekly at a public junior high near my house. Stephanie lived with her mom and her sister. Dad was an alcoholic and had been out of the picture since she was a little girl. Mom had full custody, but Dad was allowed visits.

Sadly, Dad didn't typically show up for his visits.

I remember one week inviting Stephanie and a bunch of her friends to a fun event we were holding at the school. Her friends were excited to come, but Stephanie quickly declared, "I can't. I'm hanging out with my dad that night."

Her close friends and I glanced at one another. We knew her dad's reputation. We all wondered the same thing. *Will he show up?*

The evening came and I had a break during the event. I thought of Stephanie, so I called her mom from my cell.

"Did he show?" I asked.

"Nope," she said unemotionally.

I sighed. "Where's Stephanie?"

"Waiting by the window."

I wish I could tell you this was a lone instance. I wish I could tell you this only happened to Stephanie. But sadly, over the last twenty-five years working with young people, I have seen countless young people "waiting by the window," literally and emotionally, for their parents to show up and take notice.

I remember spending considerable time with an eighth grader I'll call Todd. His dad left when he was just a baby but had visited here and there over the years. Todd was one of those kids who was allowed to do pretty much anything he wanted. His mom worked, which left him alone after school most days. He watched whatever entertainment media he desired, hung out with whoever he wanted, and never had to ask anyone permission to go anywhere. I know some entitled kids who probably think that sounds like a dream come true. But Todd would have argued to the contrary.

Once I remember making an offhanded comment to him about his parents caring for him, and Todd literally laughed out loud. "My dad doesn't give a *flip* about me!" (I'm paraphrasing.) He fought back tears.

Our kids not only want us—they need us. They need a mom and dad who notice them and make them feel valued. Much of this is from simply showing up. Much of this is from being there enough to notice when something is wrong.

The question most of you might be asking is, What does this look like—how can I find this difficult balance of loving my kids, noticing them, but not stalking them?

I have found three tools that make this practice of noticing much easier. These three tools have helped me considerably; I hope you'll find them helpful as well.

THREE ESSENTIAL TOOLS TO HELP YOU *NOTICE* YOUR KIDS

1. Duct Tape

One of the best ways parents can actually notice their kids is by merely being quiet and listening.

When I'm teaching this topic at my parenting workshops, I love to give parents an effective tool they'll remember. So I hand them each a piece of duct tape.

"Everyone place this piece of tape over your mouths. *Now* you're ready to truly engage with your kid."

The secret to better communication with our kids is learning to listen before we utter a word. I actually encourage parents to make this a game. Next time you see your kids, try something. Don't talk for ten minutes unless talked to. Instead. . .observe! You'll learn so much, it will change what you were going to say in the first place.

I was terrible at this. Whenever I walked into the room, the first thing I did was start yapping. Looking back, I think I figured, *I know what they're going through.* But I didn't.

And frankly, I knew better. I spoke to teenagers weekly. It was my job to know kids. I practiced listening first every time I was on the road. I still do.

Whenever I speak to kids at camps or events, I typically hang out with them before and after I talk. My standard routine is to casually perch myself somewhere in the room, maybe leaning up against a wall by myself. Then I do something that not many adults do.

I notice.

I literally just stand there and observe everything I can about the young people I'm about to speak to:

- What are they wearing? What does the front of their T-shirt say? Are their clothes kempt? Are they revealing? What kind of shoes did they choose?
- I notice their hair. How much time did they spend that morning getting it to look that way? Do they reach up and touch it or flip it often?
- Are they worried about the way they look? Are they glancing around to see if others are watching them?
- Do they listen more or talk more? When they listen, are they really listening, or are their eyes darting around the room to see if they're missing anything?
- Are they leaders or followers? Are people flocking to them, or are they gathering around others?
- What do they think of authority? Are they eager to see the adults around them, or are they leery of them?
- If I'm in earshot, what are they talking about? What subject perked their interest?
- What are they *not* talking about? The fine art of reading between the lines is the best practice of the wise listener. What are these kids screaming, while not actually saying out loud?

You can learn oodles about young people by just sitting and watching them. Why? Honestly, because young people aren't half as stealthy as they think they are.

Let me ask you. Have you ever taken a group of teenagers somewhere in your car? If you're smart, you just shut up and drive. Because quiet parents can learn a ton about kids if they just sit and observe.

Think about the last time you drove a group of kids. Kids will talk without thinking. They'll spill out every detail of their lives: who they like, who they dislike, what they want to buy, what they're tired of, what they saw someone post, what they posted. . .what they wish they *didn't* post. Sometimes they forget you're up there in the front seat. Occasionally you'll even hear someone in the car say something, and then your kid will quickly shush them. *Awkward silence.*

You can learn a lot—good and bad.

Again, my purpose in asking you about your listening habits is not so you will start spying on your kids or be able to bust them. My purpose is to help you understand a little more about their world.

One of the biggest complaints I hear from parents of teenagers is, "My kids won't talk with me."

As I was doing research for my book *Get Your Teenager Talking*, I asked parents what conversation in their house sounded like. The typical conversation went like this:

"How was school?"

"Fine."

"Anything exciting happen?"

"Nope."

"Got much homework?"

"A little."

"Well, better get to it."

And this was every day.

As I began working with parents, I would ask them, "Why don't you ask your kids about something they're actually interested in talking about?"

When parents were honest, they would admit, "I really don't know what my kids want to talk about."

When my daughter Alyssa was in middle school, she was very quiet around the house. She kept to herself, read, and devoted quite a bit of time to art projects. Her two siblings monopolized the dinner conversation at the table every night, and she didn't seem to mind. Most often she would just sit and listen.

Alyssa became deeply involved in her youth group at our church. One day one of the youth leaders came up to Lori and me and said, "Alyssa is so funny. Wow. She's got a lot of energy!"

Lori and I looked at each other, thinking, *You're mistaken. You must be thinking of a different Alyssa.*

Curious, I poked my head in the middle school youth room at church the next Sunday and found my daughter laughing and talking with her friends, engaged like I had truly never seen her.

I walked in and gave her a hug. She said, "Oh, hi, Dad. Let me introduce you to my friends." And bubbling with energy, she introduced me to each of her friends, offering lengthy anecdotes about them. "This is Natalie. She likes pizza so much that her family has it every Sunday after church across the street. This is Lindsey, and she has glasses like me, but she can see better than me without her glasses. . . ." She went on this way for about five minutes.

That experience opened my eyes to two things:

1. I didn't know my daughter.
2. The simple practice of observing her with her friends provided me with a wealth of talking points for the next few days.

It took me a while, but I was beginning to learn that this skill of *noticing* needed to be applied with my own family.

When moms and dads have the self-discipline to just be quiet and take notice of what is going on, they'll acquire great insight into their kids' lives, seeing firsthand what their kids get excited about, which opens the door to begin using the next tool.

2. Well-Placed Questions

Questions are the tools that keep kids talking and parents listening.

Whenever I sit down with a teenager, conversation doesn't flow easily at first. Many teens can be skeptical of adults. They don't necessarily want to peel back layers and get vulnerable.

Here's where tool number one proves imperative. If we've been disciplined enough to *silently* observe and listen, then we probably have some springboards we can use to engage this kid in conversation.

I think of it like a game. I know there is something this

kid would *love* to talk about. In fact, they probably don't get a chance to talk about it as much as they'd like, because this world is full of way more talkers than listeners. So it's my job as a caring adult to figure out what that subject is and get them talking about it.

This starts with noticing and then manifests in the form of questions.

I train youth workers how to do this in my CONNECT workshop. I tell them:

> *If a kid walks into the room wearing a Star Wars shirt, that might just be your springboard. But you need to dip your toe in the water and see. Ask them, "So, are you a true Star Wars fan, or did you just raid your dad's T-shirt drawer?"*
>
> *If he answers, "I love Star Wars! Last May I wore my Star Wars socks and Chewbacca backpack to school and got beat up three times!" then you've got something to talk about.*
>
> *On the other hand, if he answers, "Oh, I just found this shirt on the floor in my brother's room because I didn't have anything else to wear," then Star Wars probably isn't your topic, but maybe his relationship with his brother is a springboard.*

Think about what this looks like in the parenting world. Let's look at a couple of examples of noticing our kids and using what we observe as springboard questions:

You notice:

When your daughter's friends bring up the popular musician Adam Levine, your daughter becomes fully engaged. She talks about him on the TV show *The Voice*, what songs she likes, and how cute he is.

What you could ask:

1. What song is probably one of your favorite songs right now?
2. I don't know if I've heard that one—will you play it for me?
3. What is your go-to playlist this week on your phone?
4. Are any Levine songs on that list?
5. Which of his songs is probably his best ever?
6. Why do you think so many girls like Adam Levine?
7. Why do you like Adam Levine?

What you probably shouldn't ask:

1. Why do you like that old man Levine?
2. Why does he have so many disgusting tattoos?
3. Why don't you try listening to Chris Tomlin instead!

You notice:

Your son loves video games. He asks for a brand-new game you know nothing about. You see this as an opportunity to connect, so you tell him to rent it so you can play it with him. You sit down with him and ask him to teach you how to play.

What you could ask:
1. If you were locked in a room for a year with only one video game, which game would you choose? Why?
2. What game do you think most guys your age would choose? Why?
3. What is a game you really enjoy, but don't own or don't play? Why don't you play it?
4. If you were a dad, do you think you'd let your own kids play it? Explain.
5. What is the next game you want to buy?
6. Do you want to see what my favorite game was when I was your age?

What you probably shouldn't ask:
1. Why are these games all so violent?
2. How long have you been sitting on your butt playing video games today?
3. When are you going to finish your chores?

The point here is to get to know our kids. This means we are *not* asking questions so we can use their answers against them. This tactic might work once or twice, but pretty soon your kids will learn, *Hey. . .my mom's a parole officer!*

So try to ask questions with the intent of getting your kids to open up. Remember, most kids want to talk about something. It's your job to find out what that is and prove you're a safe source to talk to.

Again, avoid lectures. If you feel your kid needs to think about something, lead them to it and then ask them what they think they should do. We're actually going to spend an entire chapter looking at how parents can use questions to engage in meaningful conversations about values in "Change 6: Add a Question Mark."

Well-placed questions are very effective tools for getting to know your kids.

But today our kids exist in another world where the pressure to be noticed and accepted is at its peak. That's why parents need to have a. . .

3. Social Media Presence

Social media offers today's young people a place where they can be noticed, not only for who they actually are, but also for who they portray themselves to be in a world with no perceived accountability.

This gets a little scary when you consider that social media is sharing bandwidth with some pretty lewd elements—including the largest source of pornography available today. In fact, sometimes the line between social media and porn is blurred. I can (but won't) name several popular social media sites where young people go to "talk to strangers." If you visit their pages, it's easy to click on an "unmoderated" section where you encounter other lonely people taking off their clothes or masturbating.

Many times our kids aren't seeking out these kinds of sites; they just stumble upon them. In my book *More Than Just the Talk: Becoming Your Kids' Go-To Person about Sex*, I warn parents, "Google is the number one place young people go to for answers to their questions about sex."[5] Imagine what they are finding when they click the SEARCH button. That's why I urge parents, not just in that book but in every one of my parenting workshops, "We need to create a comfortable climate of continual conversations with our kids about these subjects so we can become their go-to person for help."

We need to be aware of what apps, websites, and social media venues our kids frequent. This is scary for a lot of parents because in many cases, our kids are more tech savvy than we are.

This isn't an excuse. We need to be engaging with our kids about their time engaging with screens. This doesn't mean spying on them. I said it earlier in this chapter: There's a fine line between noticing our kids and *stalking* our kids!

Here are a few thoughts to consider when navigating the world of social media and technology with our kids:

1. *Most parents don't monitor their kids' screen time, social media profiles, texting, etc.* A few summers ago McAfee actually did a study and found that 74 percent of parents surveyed claimed they can't possibly keep up with all their kids' entertainment media and technology, so they just simply "hope for the best."[6] So even if you decide you're going to be hands-on with your kids and involved in this area, you're in the minority. Which leads to my next thought. . .

2. *Our kids won't be excited about our efforts to walk with them through this process.* Kids want freedom. Many

of them will see our presence as a lack of trust. We need to be ready to communicate with them clearly about our desire to equip them for making decisions completely on their own. (I've devoted an entire chapter to what this looks like; see "Change 5: Segue.")

3. *Almost every expert out there encourages parents to engage in regular conversations about social media and technology.* Don't just post rules and screen-time limits (boundaries); look for opportunities to dialogue with your kids (bonding) about what they are encountering on their devices. (In fact, in the chapter "Change 6: Add a Question Mark," I'm going to introduce you to a study showing exactly what these conversations can look like.)

Keeping up with our kids' technology use is not just about finding the perfect rules or, on the other hand, letting them do whatever they want. It's much more work than either of these extremes. It's walking alongside our kids and helping them learn to discern truth in a world full of lies. (The chapter "Change 7: Walk With" will help you put feet to this goal, providing specific ideas for guardrails you can put into place.)

But sometimes when we take the time to notice our kids, we notice something worrisome. Let's take a look at some signs of trouble.

DANGER SIGNS

I don't intend to scare you, but I must raise awareness about something important.

In a world where being "liked" or accepted is believed to be so vital and significant, some of today's young people allow their insecurities to grow into an unhealthy mental state.

Suicide is actually the second leading cause of death among teenagers.[7] A surprising amount of today's young people have admitted to feeling overwhelmingly hopeless and considering suicide. Last year the Centers for Disease Control (CDC) surveyed thousands of high school students across the United States and asked them detailed questions about their feelings and behaviors.[8] One question they asked was if in the last twelve months they ever felt "sad or hopeless almost every day for two weeks or more"—so much so that they "stopped doing some usual activities." A remarkable 40 percent of females identified with this description, as did 20 percent of males.

The CDC went on to ask questions specifically about suicide. They asked students if, in the last twelve months, they had. . .

Seriously considered attempting suicide:
GUYS   23%
GIRLS   12%

Made a plan for how they would do it:
GUYS   19%
GIRLS   10%

Attempted suicide:
GUYS   12%
GIRLS   6%

In many of these circumstances, the parents didn't have a clue. In most of these situations, the parents didn't *notice*.

Some of you might be wondering if you have missed some of these warning signs. You might be thinking, *What if my kid is displaying signs of severe anxiety or depression?*

How can we tell if our kids are slipping under the radar and engaging in harmful behaviors?

Allow me to comfort you. If you invest time in your kids' lives, the chances are you'll *notice*! Again, the best way to be aware is by being involved in your kids' lives, noticing them, listening to them, and interacting with them about their thoughts, feelings, and opinions. If you start to notice some questionable changes in your child's friends, habits, or attitude, these could be signs of something deeper going on.

Here are some signs that might prompt you to engage in deeper conversations about what you observe:

- Withdrawal from family and friends
- Loss of interest in hobbies and activities
- Bad grades or progress reports from school
- Not eating or severe changes in diet
- Change in wardrobe or even wearing apparel that doesn't make sense (e.g., a long-sleeve shirt on a hot summer day)
- Inability to sleep
- Extreme irritability or angry outbursts
- Self-deprecating comments about oneself
- Extreme sadness or loneliness

Don't be worried if you see one of these signs on occasion. Some of these changes occur with adolescence. Teens can grow more emotional when puberty kicks in, and as you probably remember, middle school and high school can be rough environments. Consider some of the struggles and feelings you had when you were that age.

If you do notice something worrisome, don't be afraid to reach out to your child's teachers, coaches, youth leaders, and other caring adults to ask if they've noticed anything. Sometimes our kids will be more transparent in other environments.

If you or other caring adults see several of these signs happening frequently, don't be afraid to address your concerns calmly and compassionately. Maybe ask, "Yesterday I asked you if something was wrong and you said no. But I can tell something's going on. Don't worry; you're not in trouble. I just want to understand. Maybe I can help."

If you hear talk that's a little disconcerting, don't be afraid to ask tough questions like, "Are you feeling hopeless? Have you maybe thought of hurting yourself or others?" But don't just ask yes-or-no questions. Ask a question like, "What are you feeling?" And then be quiet and listen.

This conversation should come from a place of love and concern. Never demand they tell you what's wrong. Assure them you love them and will do whatever it takes to help them.

Don't ask these questions if your kids aren't showing any of the signs. They'll quickly tire of this kind of dialogue. In other words. . .

DON'T OVERREACT

Please, don't panic. If you see a school shooting in the news, it doesn't mean it's time to search your kids' room for bombs. And when you read an article about "sexting," you don't need to demand to see your kids' phones when they walk in the door. Your day-to-day interaction with your kids will provide you with the best pulse as to what's going on in their lives.

Let me encourage you by telling you honestly one of the most depressing facts I have observed. Parents don't do this! They don't *notice.*

Why?

It takes a lot of time and energy.

I understand. When I finish a long day at work and finally sit down in my recliner and put my feet up. . .well, that option is much more relaxing than walking upstairs to my kids' rooms, plopping on the floor next to them where they're watching Netflix, and asking, "Whatcha watching? Mind if I join you?"

But when I do the latter, I rarely regret it.

Notice. Listen. Encourage.

Most kids love being heard—they're just never given the opportunity. What can you do to truly notice your kids today?

LIVING IT OUT THIS WEEK

QUESTIONS TO DISCUSS WITH YOUR SPOUSE AND/OR OTHER PARENTS

1. What is one thing in this chapter that made you think?
2. What are some ways you see today's young people expressing the longing, "Notice me"?
3. How has social media magnified the desire to fit in?
4. What are some ways today's parents can notice their kids, without stalking?
5. Describe a time when you listened before you talked and it paid off.
6. Jonathan mentioned that it's hard to "get teenagers talking" when we don't talk about something they're interested in. What are some topics your kids might be interested in talking about?
7. What are some questions you might be able to ask your kids about this topic?
8. What is one thing you read in this chapter that you would like to implement this week? When will you try it?

CHANGE 4

PRESS PAUSE

Two chapters ago I introduced the principle of "letting it go" and not becoming argumentative, especially as our kids grow and vie for independence. Don't be fooled into thinking picking our battles is the same as "pressing pause" on our anger. Out-of-control anger can grow into a monster destroying everything in its path. Pressing pause is a vital practice that deserves its very own chapter.

Nothing hurt my relationship with my kids more than my angry outbursts.

Nothing!

But not many people know this, because most of us who struggle with our temper keep our ugly outbursts under the radar.

My daughter Ashley loves watching family videos. Now that she's in college, it's not uncommon for her to pull out a family video and pop it in when she's home for the summer or a holiday. We'll all sit on the couch and laugh and reminisce.

"Do you remember that trip? That was so much fun!"

"I forgot about that toy! I loved my Littlest Pet Shop!"

"Dad. . .where did you get those shorts? Those were terrible!"

We were one of those families who had the video

camera out a lot when the kids were young. We captured all kinds of great memories. Whenever I watch our old family videos, I'm filled with blissful memories of time together as a family.

Funny. . .those videos didn't capture everything.

The camera wasn't typically on when one of the kids was disobeying. The camera wasn't recording when Lori and I would get into a disagreement. And the camera certainly wasn't on anytime I reached the boiling point and opted to yell to get the result I wanted.

Sadly, my family probably doesn't need to see any footage to recall these moments. They remember them crystal clear. Moments like that make permanent impressions.

It's hard to minimize the effect of losing your temper. Those of us who lose our cool often would love to diminish the damage each explosion causes, but sadly, every blast leaves fragments of shrapnel and a dark cloud of smoke throughout our home. And everyone knows smoke leaves a permanent smell no matter how hard you try to wash it out.

I wish I would have foreseen the damage my angry outbursts could cause.

Angry outbursts teach our kids, *I can't go to Mom. She'll freak out.* Or *Dad isn't safe.*

Consider the ramifications of that feeling. If Mom or Dad isn't safe, then whose arms will our kids run to for comfort, for advice. . .for admiration? There's no denying it: uncontrolled anger affects our kids' self-esteem, their confidence, and their entire worldview.

There is nothing I regret more than the times I lost my temper in my home.

In a very forthright article, Michelle J. Watson, PhD, shared what she described as the most important advice she would give dads: "Stop venting your anger at your daughter."[1]

In the article she described what anger does to young girls, using descriptions like "destroys her spirit," "makes her shut down," and "crushes" her. But then she gave what I thought was the most compelling reason dads need to control their temper: "Remember, Dad, that you are modeling for her the way that she should expect to be treated by a guy she dates and a guy she one day will marry."

Ouch!

That thought terrified me, especially as a parent of two daughters! I'd hate to think that my girls would settle for mediocrity someday because I taught them that uncontrolled anger is no big deal.

It's a tough pill for parents to swallow: our actions have serious repercussions in our kids' lives. Sadly, when we're angry, our kids typically react in one of two ways: they internalize it or they imitate it. Neither is good.

The kid who internalizes it holds it all inside. When Mom or Dad is angry, little Taylor doesn't say a word. She tries her hardest to do anything she can to just make the anger go away. She desperately wants to make peace. Unfortunately, this only works temporarily. Usually these feelings will either build up and explode or seep into other areas of her life and wreak havoc.

The polar opposite reaction is the kid who expresses these feelings in his everyday life. Little Brandon yells back, because that's what he's been taught. Outside the house he mimics Mom's or Dad's lack of self-control, whining and complaining at everything that doesn't go his way. These actions help Brandon feel better about himself. In fact, when he gets mad at others, it's a chance to raise himself up since he feels dejected and squashed by his own mom or dad.

I can't even count how many times in my last twenty-plus years of youth ministry I encountered adolescent bullies who, once I met their parents, I quickly realized were only acting out and trying to elevate themselves because they were crushed by their parents every day.

By God's grace, I wasn't one of those parents. But my record is far from clean. There were far too many times when out of frustration or even sheer exhaustion I opted to yell when my kids misbehaved.

I recently had lunch with a close friend of mine who has young teens. He was asking me for advice about his oldest son who was pushing his buttons. I referenced some of the research I was conducting for this book and talked about the effect of anger on our kids. Our two families went on many family trips together when my kids were teens and his boys were just toddlers, so we know each other pretty well. I confessed, "You probably remember some of the times when I lost my cool. I wish I could have handled some of those situations differently."

His reply was intriguing. He said, "I do remember some of those moments, and at the time I remember thinking sometimes you were a little harsh." He leaned in close to me. "But then my kids became teenagers, and now I completely understand and I'm right there with you!"

There's no denying it. Teenagers' behavior can be very frustrating!

I think many parents are unprepared for exactly how difficult parenting is going to be.

You Will Be Angry

I began teaching parenting workshops when my kids were young. I had worked with teenagers for over a decade at the time, done extensive social research, and become one of the go-to sources about youth culture, writing articles and teaching at conventions and conferences. If someone sat in one of my parenting workshops, they heard the experience of a parent of young children and someone who knew teenagers well.

Then my own kids turned into teenagers. . .*and everything changed*!

In all honesty, what I was missing was the experience of parenting *my own* teenagers! There's something different about having teenagers of your own and being entrusted with the responsibility of raising them 24/7. Parenting teenagers is a whole different ball game than parenting toddlers!

Parenting toddlers is *physically* tiring.

"Daddy, will you play with me?"

"Daddy, Alyssa took my crayon."

"Daddy, I think I had an accident in my big-boy pants."

Parents of young kids are constantly on the move. Changing diapers, rolling on the floor, playing pretend, feeding them, cleaning them, bathing them, helping them do virtually everything!

Parenting teenagers is *emotionally* exhausting. Sure, they can dress themselves and fix themselves lunch. . .but the drama!

"That's so unfair! All my friends are allowed to do it!"

"Mom, your music stinks! Please put on anything else!"

"Why do you care what I wear? Everyone is wearing these kinds of tops!"

It's tiring. Sometimes they win battles merely by wearing you down. They've mastered the war of attrition.

Ever since I had teenagers of my own, my parenting workshops have morphed. The biggest change? Humility. Now I teach workshops as a fellow battered parent!

Teenagers are the biggest blow to a person's self-esteem. One of my friends proofing this book told me, "I'm not sure I knew what real humility was until I suffered through the tween/teenage years with my daughter."

So many teenagers are inherently rude. I can't believe the way I hear today's teenagers talk to their parents.

"Whatever."

"Just sayin'!"

Respect for one's elders is slowly becoming extinct.

Today's young people *will* make you angry. So be prepared. Even the nicest kids will say the meanest things. . .unintentionally.

Honestly, I think it happens through sheer osmosis. Today's tweens and teens live in a me-focused culture where everything is handed to them, and where most of the satire they hear is self-seeking, insolent, and mocking. It's hard for anyone to live a respectful life in such a disrespectful culture.

Not to mention, when your kids become teenagers, they don't know squat about life, but they think they know everything! So prepare yourself. You'll be lucky if you can get through the day without someone one-third your age telling you how you should live your life!

Your kids will definitely make you angry. Your spouse will make you angry. It's part of life. We can't control other people's words and actions.

Dr. Willard Harley Jr. notes this reality in his book *Love Busters*, specifically in his chapter about angry outbursts. He writes, "The truth is, there are many situations in life, especially in marriage, where we cannot make others do what we want them to. People will do irritating things, there's no getting around it."[2]

You will get angry. The question is, how will you respond?

Your Choice

Anger isn't wrong.

Anger can actually be a very good thing. People throughout history have become angry for very good reasons. Anger began powerful movements stopping injustices. The Bible is clear that even God gets angry. Anger in itself is not a sin. "Uncontrolled anger" is what we need to be careful of.

In other words, when you feel angry, what are you going to do about it?

I've read countless articles, chapters, even entire books on anger. Many experts jump straight to how to avoid losing control. I'm not knocking them—I'm even going to provide you with a few tips that have helped me. But first, we all need to understand something even more vital: *We have a choice about how we respond.*

I'm amazed how I allowed myself to react in the past.

Key words: *I allowed.*

It's true. Whenever I lost my temper, it was because I gave in to the desire to lose control. It was the easy road. Instead of disciplining myself to exhibit self-control, I chose to go with what felt good at the moment.

Sure, some people might protest, "But I can't help it."

That's entirely false. And I can prove it. Have you ever been in the middle of a huge fight at home where voices are raised, and then you receive an important phone call? Your voice changes completely.

I remember moments like this in my house, when voices were raised to the max:

"HOW COULD YOU EVEN *THINK* THAT!"

"EASY! YOU WERE BEING MEAN!"

"*I'M* BEING MEAN? LOOK AT *YOU!*"

Ring. . .ring.

"Hello, the McKee residence."

Our anger is controllable. Some of us simply allow it because there's no accountability. How will anyone know if we yell at our family? Yelling doesn't leave any physical marks. That almost makes it allowable.

Let that sink in for a moment. Are the following actions acceptable?

- Hitting your kids
- Cheating on your spouse
- Pulling out a gun and shooting someone
- Yelling out racial slurs

Of course not! These actions will lead to jail, divorce, unemployment, and possibly even getting beat to death!

Then let me ask a rather obvious question: Why is it okay to yell at your kids and crush them emotionally, but not to hit them in the jaw? Clinically, it's called verbal abuse. Yes. . .*abuse*. And it should be as off-limits as hitting our kids or any of these other actions. So why do we allow it?

My point is simple. If you have the self-control to refrain from hitting your kid, or having an affair—because those actions are off-limits—then you can exert the same control and not yell at your kids. Each of us has the ability to exercise self-control. We prove it in many other areas of our lives. (Sadly, if we don't, then we might just end up divorced, in jail, unemployed, etc.) We need to apply self-control to our anger, because out-of-control anger has dire consequences.

Which is more powerful—your tongue or your fist?

Have you ever said words you wish you could take back?

Words are permanent. . .*and memorable*. Many of us can probably recall instances when we said something regrettable in the heat of the moment, only to wish we could take those words back the second they escaped our lips.

My dad and I teach workshops for new managers in the corporate world. In these workshops we sometimes lead discussions about how to express anger toward employees or customers.

In one of these workshops my dad opened up discussion around the question, "When you lose control of your emotions and yell out your feelings, is it really how you feel?" The discussion was lively as the managers argued both sides of the issue. After they discussed it for some time, my dad made the point that most often when you lose your cool and express your anger in heated comments, it is how you feel at the moment, but not necessarily how you really feel. The key words were *at the moment*.

A woman in the class spoke up and shared how recently she was so angry with her son, she yelled, "I wish you would go live with your father." She broke down as she shared. She confessed that at that moment she was so mad she felt like killing him, but the second she said those words, she regretted them and tried to take them back. She kept apologizing to her son and telling him she didn't mean it, but it was too late. The words were out there. He moved in with his father.

Angry outbursts inflict permanent damage *if* we allow them in our lives.

The choice is yours. Are you going to give uncontrolled anger free rein in your home?

ACTUALLY DEFEATING ANGRY OUTBURSTS

I probably don't have to spend any more time convincing you angry outbursts are unhealthy and can wreak havoc in your home. The question many of us more likely have is "How can I avoid these outbursts when I'm in the situation?"

It's easy for me to tell you, "Stop getting angry." The more difficult question is "How do I stop getting angry?" What does it actually look like when your kids are being disrespectful and yelling seems like the only viable option to straighten them out?

I've been there! I've failed in the heat of the moment more times than I can count.

There's that key phrase again, *in the moment*.

I'm not always very wise *in the moment*.

And that's why pressing pause is soooo important! The simple act of pressing pause suppresses stupidity.

It's like this: when we're angry, we aren't thinking clearly. Never give the microphone to someone who isn't thinking clearly. (Many of you have learned this firsthand when your drunk uncle gave a toast at your wedding.) If you're like me, you'll need time to think. How many times have you responded quickly and then looked back at the situation later and thought, *if only I would have said. . .?*

Well, we don't have a *do-over button. . .*we have something much better! A *pause button.* A pause button allows you to take the same kind of time to think over your actions. . .*but before you do them!* Instead of lying in a bed of regret and imagining how you would do things differently if you had a do-over, pause for a moment and consider those same ramifications before you act in the first place!

Pressing pause is comprised of three key elements.

THREE KEY ELEMENTS OF PRESSING PAUSE
1. The Delay

The pause button is magical for one reason: *the delay.*

What's the most common advice you hear people give to help control your temper?

Count to ten.

I remember trying that. Ten was never enough. I might as well have counted backward—a countdown to the explosion.

Counting to ten is solid advice when ten means minutes. . . or hours. The key is taking time to think before you act.

Delay!

This is truly a discipline. It's hard! When your kids talk back or disobey, it takes incredible strength to press pause and delay your response. Especially if you're like me, the type of person who wants to deal with a situation immediately. I don't like leaving things undone. I want to solve problems now! It's against my nature to delay my response.

But failure after failure taught me: acting immediately never solved anything. Delaying my response was always a better choice.

Let's be real: our first thoughts aren't always our best thoughts. They're usually filled with unprocessed emotion and ignorance. Time allows us to sort our thoughts and process information. It's amazing how much smarter you will be ten, twenty. . .sixty minutes later!

So press pause and delay your reaction. If your son or daughter messes up, take a deep breath and then calmly say: "Emily, I need to think about this. Go to your room and start on your homework, and I'm going to take some time to figure out what we're going to do. I'll call you down in an hour or two—or maybe next Tuesday."

If you are really tempted to make your kids pay immediately for what they've done, then take small pleasure in the fact that delaying the situation is actually a discipline itself. Kids hate waiting for punishments!

This strategy works well with kids of all ages. I remember when my brother and I got in trouble as kids while our dad was at work. The worst punishment my mom ever gave was when she calmly walked in the room and said, "I've had enough. Each of you go to your room and just wait until your father gets home!"

"Aaaargh!"

It was the worst punishment we could ever be dealt.
Wait for your unknown punishment.

"Please! Not that! Can you just beat us with a lead pipe instead?"

After blowing it with my kids countless times, I began adopting this principle of pressing pause, and the result was truly miraculous! Not only did it provide me with the much-needed time to think it over; it drove my kids nuts! They actually told me, "Can you just yell at me so we can get it all over with?"

Pardon my alliteration, but pressing pause provides you with a period to produce proper perspective.

In 1870 John D. Rockefeller founded Standard Oil, a corporation that became one of the world's first and largest multinational corporations. The company acquired and developed some of the greatest leaders and decision makers of that time, but not all of them were perfect.

One day, one of those senior executives made a wrong decision that cost the company more than two million dollars. Most of the other executives avoided Rockefeller that day, giving him some time to cool off. But one man, Edward T. Bedford, a partner in the company, kept his appointment with Rockefeller.

When he entered the office, Bedford recalls seeing the powerful head of the empire leaning over his desk writing on a pad of paper. After a few minutes, Rockefeller looked up.

"Oh, it's you, Bedford," he said calmly. "I suppose you've heard about our loss?"

Bedford acknowledged that he had.

"I've been thinking it over," Rockefeller said, "and before I ask the man in to discuss the matter, I've been making some notes."

Bedford told the story like this:

> *Across the top of the page was written, "Points in favor of Mr. _____." There followed a long list of the man's virtues, including a brief description of how he had helped the company make the right decision on three separate occasions that had earned many times the cost of his recent error.*
>
> *I never forgot that lesson. In later years, whenever I was tempted to rip into anyone, I forced myself first to sit down and thoughtfully compile as long a list of good points as I possibly could. Invariably, by the time I finished my inventory, I would see the matter in its true perspective and keep my temper under control. There is no telling how many times this habit has prevented me from committing one of the costliest mistakes any executive can make— losing his temper. I commend it to anyone who must deal with people.[3]*

Pressing pause provides enough delay for the voice of wisdom to be heard.

2. A Soft Voice

When I was doing research for this book, the words I kept encountering were "gentle" and "soft approach." Many therapists talk specifically about your voice. "Soften your voice. Look into their eyes. Make them feel heard."

It's amazing how much better my kids responded when I used a soft voice.

It's counterintuitive—I agree. Yelling gets us quick results.

That's why I did it. When my kids disobeyed and I was too tired to get to the bottom of it, a quick bark would set them straight. . .so I thought. What I actually did was train them to listen *only* to loud instructions. People do this with their dogs. They yell to get results.

What do dogs do when you yell at them?

They cower.

Do you want kids who cower when you enter the room?

My cousin lives on a nine-hundred-acre ranch and at any given time has over one hundred head of cattle in one of his pastures. His dog of choice is a border collie. This is no ordinary pet—this is a working dog.

Whenever we go on a walk, his dog is right at his heels. As we enter a meadow with cows, the dog is eager to work. It's hilarious to watch. Border collies all have OCD. They can't stand to see cows spread out in disorder. They want them all tucked into one nice spot.

After making his dog wait for a few minutes, practically bursting out of his furry little skull, my cousin will finally whisper, "Go to work."

The second he utters those barely audible words, the

dog springs into action and begins rounding up cows.

That's when it gets truly amazing.

Even though the dog is about one hundred yards away, my cousin will speak in a soft voice, the same volume as if he were talking to someone right next to him.

"Come."

Every time, the dog immediately stops in his tracks, turns, and sprints back to his master.

I looked at my kids and said, "Why can't you do that?"

Funny, we've all seen dog owners yelling at their dogs because their dogs aren't listening. And we've all seen parents yelling at their kids because their kids aren't listening.

How have we *conditioned* our kids to respond?

I've worked with some pretty tough teenagers in my decades of youth ministry, and it didn't take me long to realize that yelling doesn't work. In fact, I remember I once yelled at a kid and he gave me a look that said, "I might just stab you."

Yelling reminded this kid of his dad. He *hated* his dad!

Do you know what commanded these kids' respect?

Respect.

If I gave respect, I often received respect in return.

It's simple: the more we yell, the less they listen. When we use a loud voice, our attempt to instruct is worthless because we have proven to be a worthless instructor.

A gentle approach and a soft voice go miles in our parenting efforts.

Don't get me wrong. I'm not telling you to let your kids walk all over you. I'm not hinting that you should have no rules or guidelines. Far from it. The soft and gentle is all about *how* we should talk while setting those guidelines.

The book of Proverbs gives some relevant advice in this regard: "A gentle answer turns away wrath, but a harsh word stirs up anger" (15:1).

Consider what that might look like in your house. When we're angry, our kids get stirred up to respond negatively. Anger leads to more anger.

That's not very smart.

A gentle answer might be the approach you're looking for.

3. God's Power

One of the worst mistakes we can make parenting is to try to accomplish great results on our own. That's called pride. The reality is, we need help. And there's one source of help that will provide you with all the strength you need in your role as a parent.

I've heard countless parenting sermons where someone reads this verse from the Bible: "Fathers, do not exasperate your children; instead, bring them up in the training and instruction of the Lord" (Ephesians 6:4).

Some scholars will dive into the original Greek word for "exasperate"—*parorgizō*—define it (to provoke, arouse to anger), and show the three times it is used in the New Testament. The point of all these sermons is always something like, "Hey, moms and dads, don't frustrate your kids by giving in to your own urges. Bring them up in truth."

I've heard the sermon probably a hundred times. And every time I'm sitting there in the audience thinking, *Tell me how!*

No one ever answers *how*. And it's a shame, because the

answer is there if you read the whole book of Ephesians. Ephesians was a letter, and it was meant to be read in its entirety.

The same problem exists when someone talks about marriage. Whenever someone preaches on marriage, you can almost bet they're going to open up the book of Ephesians to chapter 5, verses 21–28, the famous part of scripture where Paul instructs husbands and wives that they should be "submit[ting] to one another out of reverence for Christ" (verse 21).

These verses also don't tell us where to get the strength to do this. Anyone who has been married or had kids knows that both relationships can be very difficult. We don't need someone simply telling us, "Do it better." The more helpful advice would be telling us *how to do it*. After all, the world is full of distractions trying to mislead us and tell us to live for ourselves and just do what feels good at the moment. The book of Ephesians reminds us that we aren't to live like this. Instead, we need to let the Holy Spirit take over.

So what's the secret?

Not our *own* power. . .but His power *in us*.

Think about this concept. If Paul were standing here giving us marriage or parenting advice today, he might lay it all out like this:

> *"Why don't you stop trying to live like the world and what the media is telling you to do? They are so confused. Their minds are twisted and they live for the moment, stuff like lustful pleasure. . .need I go on?*

"But that's not you! You have Jesus, right? If you are not one of those people who just says you're a Christian but instead are a true follower of Christ, then you live out the truth. You don't pursue those old selfish desires; instead, you allow Christ's influence to lead you. So continue to immerse yourself in Christ, getting to know Him better so you live like Him!"

Wouldn't it be cool if he said that to us, just like that?

Funny. . .Paul did say that, just a little bit before the marriage and parenting advice in Ephesians. In fact, what you just read was my paraphrase of his words. Read his real words:

With the Lord's authority I say this: Live no longer as the Gentiles do, for they are hopelessly confused. Their minds are full of darkness; they wander far from the life God gives because they have closed their minds and hardened their hearts against him. They have no sense of shame. They live for lustful pleasure and eagerly practice every kind of impurity.

But that isn't what you learned about Christ. Since you have heard about Jesus and have learned the truth that comes from him, throw off your old sinful nature and your former way of life, which is corrupted by lust and deception. Instead, let the Spirit renew your thoughts and attitudes. Put on your new nature,

created to be like God—truly righteous and holy.
(4:17–24 NLT)

There it is. Get rid of the old way (the old sinful nature), and instead let the Spirit renew your thoughts and attitudes.

When we look back at Ephesians as a whole, we realize that marriage and parenting are just two more areas of our lives where we allow God to fill us. Paul is helping us understand that when we allow God's Spirit to transform us, our relationships will be transformed as well.

So what does this look like?

It means that every helpful tip in this book won't do any good if you aren't humbling yourself and saying, "God, I need Your help. I need to focus on Your way, not mine."

If self-control is one of your struggles, perhaps you need to start each day soaking in some truth before you embark into a world so full of lies. Start with the book of Ephesians in the Bible, if you want. Or start reading about Jesus in Matthew or Mark. Pray before you read and ask God, "Speak truth to me today through Your Word." And after you read it, ask Him, "God, help me apply this truth today with my family, my friends, and my coworkers."

Jesus said, "Apart from me you can do nothing" (John 15:5). Don't try this parenting thing on your own—especially if you have teenagers! You'll need all the help you can get.

The simple practice of pressing pause—*delay, use a soft voice,* and *tap into God's power*—has helped me immensely in fighting the battle against angry outbursts. I hope it helps you, too.

Many of us might want to step back and ask an even deeper question: Why am I repeatedly lashing out in anger? Another effective way of dealing with anger is identifying the source of the anger and attempting to remove it.

If you battle with anger, ask yourself, Why am I angry? Are you under too much stress? If so. . .

- You may need to lighten your load. That might mean saying no to certain activities.
- Set boundaries for yourself. Don't put yourself in situations that cause you stress. (It's amazing how much stress is self-inflicted.)
- Exercise. Exercise is a proven stress reliever.
- Get rid of guilt! Confession is good for the soul. If you are carrying a burden because of something you've done, talk with someone about it. Ask for forgiveness. God is ready to give you a clean slate and a fresh start (1 John 1:9).

Are your kids undisciplined and huge sources of frustration in your life? If so. . .

- Consider reading some parenting articles and/or books about discipline and boundaries (both can be found at TheSource4Parents.com).
- Talk with other parents and share your frustrations. Ask them what works in their home.
- Attend parenting workshops where you can glean some helpful tips about balancing bonding and boundaries in your home.

And in any of these situations, don't be embarrassed if you feel you need to seek some professional help. A professional counselor can help you identify problems and set realistic remedies.

LIVING IT OUT THIS WEEK

QUESTIONS TO DISCUSS WITH YOUR SPOUSE AND/OR OTHER PARENTS

1. What is one thing in this chapter that jumped out at you?
2. What damage have you seen as the result of angry outbursts?
3. Why do you think angry outbursts have such lasting consequences?
4. Why do you think some people allow verbal abuse but not physical abuse?
5. What are some of the benefits of pressing pause and giving yourself a delay? Give an example of what this might look like during a tense moment in your home.
6. How does a soft answer turn away wrath?
7. What does Jonathan mean by "tapping into God's power"? What would that look like in your life?
8. What is one thing you read in this chapter that you would like to implement this week? When will you try it?

CHANGE 5

SEGUE

When my kids were in middle school, I heard something repeatedly from my kids. "Dad, none of my friends' parents are this strict."

Name the topic:

> *Their phones:* I had more rules.
> *Their music:* I was more involved in what
>   they listened to.
> *Their screen time:* We monitored it much
>   more than most of their friends' parents.

And I don't regret any of it.

Yes, I realize this book is about parenting practices I would do *differently* if I had a do-over. And truly, I would *not* change the guardrails I placed for my kids in middle school. I think my rules were on par.

The part I'd change is the *segue*.

No, I'm not talking about one of those cool little two-wheeled motor carts that mall cops ride. I'm talking about an actual segue—decreasing one thing while increasing another.

Remember at your high school junior prom when they faded out the song "Thriller" while fading in "Endless

Love"? You could still hear Michael Jackson's beat fading while Lionel Ritchie's entrancing piano score began. DJs are the master of the segue, and a good DJ knows how to segue from one song to another seamlessly. Parents need to learn the same skill—gradually decreasing the boundaries they set for their kids while gradually increasing their freedom to make decisions.

I wish I would have implemented this strategy from the beginning.

Here's what I mean.

When I first had kids, I didn't really have a game plan. The ball was hiked and we just began running. I hadn't thought through the amount of guidance my kids would need at different ages, and I had never really thought through the need for different degrees of help from Dad and Mom. I was just strict because I thought that would help my kids learn the difference between right and wrong. But soon they grew to the age where they needed to learn how to make moral decisions when Dad and Mom weren't there.

How can our kids learn to make these decisions if Mom and Dad keep making decisions for them?

Or let me ask another question: *When is the magic age?*

We've all wondered how long to keep on the training wheels. *When can my daughter spend the night at her friend's house? When should I let my son have his first phone?*

First consider the big picture. No one would argue with the fact that toddlers need a lot of guidance. If you take your kids camping and your two-year-old starts running toward the campfire, I don't know many parents who would just sit there and say, "Let him learn his lesson the hard way!" Parents recognize toddlers require plenty of guidance!

On the opposite extreme, when our kids get to age eighteen, they can pack their bags, move out, and join the Marines. We don't set their bedtime anymore. We don't have control over what apps they download. At this point we don't set the rules. A drill sergeant does.

Are all eighteen-year-olds ready to make decisions on their own? Sadly, no. But the reality is, when our kids are eighteen, they *can* legally move out, get their own place, and begin making all their own choices.

The point of debate is always the time in between age two and eighteen. Some parents stay strict until the day their kids leave (I gravitated this way with my oldest). Other parents don't provide any guidance at all, even when their kids need it.

When do you plan to let your kids start learning to make their own decisions?

I had never thought this through with my oldest. When he was in middle school, I was very involved in all his decisions. Name it:

- Junk food intake
- Screen time
- Chores
- Homework
- Bedtime
- Curfew

Kids are still pretty immature in middle school and aren't ready to make these decisions on their own. I didn't leave it up to my twelve-year-old to decide if he wanted to eat Cocoa Puffs for breakfast every morning, watch HBO into the late hours, and go to bed at 2:00 a.m. Twelve-year-olds would probably make bad decisions in all three of those areas.

But then he turned thirteen. . .

and fourteen. . .

and fifteen. . .

Soon he turned sixteen, got his driver's license and a job, and began looking at colleges. And I hadn't backed off. I still monitored his homework, his screen time, his chores, his bedtime. . .

In less than two years he would be in a dorm making all these decisions completely on his own, and I still wasn't giving him any practice making decisions.

I was shortsighted really. I had never asked myself, *When do I plan to let him make some of these choices on his own?*

Sure, he had a little more freedom than he did in junior high. We let him stay up later, and we let him have more screen time. Key words: we *let him*. We told him he was getting older and taking on more responsibility, but the truth is, we were still missing an important parenting principle: *incremental independence.*

We were the ones still making all of those decisions for him!

So as my daughters were entering adolescence, Lori and I made a drastic change in our parenting practices. In fact, I announced it to them when they were entering high school. I told them, "By the time you turn seventeen and a half, you won't have any rules. Not one!"

Funny. . .they didn't complain.

When they were thirteen years old, they had thought I was on the strict side. "Dad! Brianna's mom lets us do that!"

So that's when I told them, "For the next couple of years, you might think we're strict. We might even appear more strict than some of your friends' parents. But by the time you're a senior in high school, your friends are going to think you have the coolest parents in the world. . .*because you won't have any rules.*"

Some of my friends thought I was nuts. "Jonathan, that's crazy! What if your daughter wants to stay out all night and party?"

Really? Should we wait until our kids are eighteen years old or out of the house to let them have their first try at making decisions for themselves?

Pause and think about that for a moment. If we've done our job as parents, teaching our kids strong values, helping them develop discernment, giving them more and more responsibility as they've gotten older, then our senior in high school will need very little guidance at this point anyway. Besides, our kids are legally free to do whatever they want at age eighteen, so we might as well set them up to win and let 'em have a trial run while we're still there to pick 'em up when they fall.

This is what I called "the segue." And I'm not alone.

Last year, in a North Point Web interview, Andy Stanley talked about the difficult task of raising middle school kids.

Stanley, the pastor of North Point Community Church in Atlanta, speaks to parents and leaders worldwide and has written some of the most insightful leadership books I've read in the last twenty years.

In this particular interview he was asked, " 'Begin with the end in mind.' What do you mean by that?"

Stanley answered:

> *We heard something early on in our parenting that really was a defining moment. The general principle was, when it came to disciplining kids in general, you start super, super narrow and you over time give greater and greater freedom. So when we hit middle school. . .I sat down with our kids and said, "Let me tell you what our goal for you is. Our goal is that you will have no rules and no curfew." And of course they [lit] up. "So our goal is to lighten up as soon as we can, because as soon as you're showing responsibility, we'll give you more responsibility and more freedom."[1]*

Consider what great news this is for our kids! Just when they're beginning to wonder why they don't have some of the same freedoms their friends presently have, Mom and Dad reveal a very promising future.

Sure, *strict rules now* isn't the greatest news. But the hope of freedom!

Stanley says it so well. He told his kids:

> *"We don't really want to parent you. What that means is, in the short term, you might have more rules and less freedom than some of your friends,*

but in the end you are going to have fewer rules
and more freedom than some of your friends. We
want you to have the same freedom you have
your freshman year of college while you are at
home with us."

When I gave my girls this speech years prior (though probably not as eloquently as Andy Stanley), they had no objections.

It was surprising, honestly. I thought they were going to whine about how strict I was in the present. But they didn't. They seemed to appreciate the fact that their mom and dad's plan for the future was to give them freedom. They saw freedom as earned, not given.

REAL-WORLD RULES

Consider what this looks like in the real world.

First, remember what you've read so far in this book. This chapter has been focusing on boundaries. Even though I'm advising you to be strict with your kids when they're young, this doesn't negate a word I've said about the importance of bonding. So don't make the mistake I confessed early in the book in "Change 1: Tip the Scales" when my focus on the perfect *boundaries* actually sabotaged my *bonding*! Boundaries are very important, but not at the expense of bonding. So keep searching for those venues of connection with your kids. Remember that values are often passed down during bonding time even more so than when you're setting your kids' curfew.

Finding the balance between boundaries and bonding

requires us to pick our battles, as we learned in "Change 2: Let It Go." It's inevitable. Our kids will come home, skip their chores, and put their dirty feet up on the kitchen table while eating junk food and blasting loud music through their headphones. You'll have to make on-the-spot decisions about which battles are worth fighting. When they're young, be strict. When they're older, remember real-world consequences speak louder.

These decisions are easier when you take the time to get to know your kid like we learned about in "Change 3: Notice." You'll make much wiser and more informed decisions when you invest the time to listen and silently observe.

Then—and only then—consider setting guidelines.

Imagine your eleven-year-old insists on getting her own smartphone. After all, "All my friends have one!" What's the right decision?

The first thing you should do is research the answer. For many of us, that means going to Google and typing in, "What age should kids get smartphones?" Your inquiry could quite possibly bring you to one of our "Youth Culture Window" articles on our website, TheSource4Parents.com, like the recent article appropriately titled " 'Can I Have a Phone?' Answering Every Kid's Burning Question."[2] In that article you will read how most experts recommend kids *do not* begin using social media until age thirteen.[3] Most social media platforms require kids to be thirteen to sign up because of the Children's Online Privacy Protection Act (COPPA), which prevents sites from collecting select information from kids under thirteen. Parents who allow their kids to sign up on these platforms before then are allowing them to lie about their age.

I think you'll find a little research is quite helpful for making these decisions.

Once you decide what's best, shrewdly communicate your decision to your child. Give them the big picture: "Our goal is for you to make all these decisions on your own by the time you get to your senior year of high school. So our job now is to teach you good discernment so you gain plenty of experience making good choices by the time you're making these choices yourself."

Then explain to them about COPPA and how kids under age thirteen aren't supposed to be posting to Instagram or Snapchat. Let them know that they need to demonstrate maturity and trustworthiness so they can get their own phone at age thirteen and begin learning how to use some of these apps responsibly.

Once they get their own phone, segue from rigid rules to flexible freedom. The older they get, the more trust and responsibility they earn.

What might this look like?

Here's just a sample. You may choose to be more rigid or flexible. The important element to observe is the incremental independence:

Music
- When they are ten years old, they can only listen to music from the family playlists.
- When they are thirteen, they can download their own playlists on their own device, but they ask permission before downloading any song.

- When they are fifteen, they not only can have their own playlists but can download music without asking permission. But Mom and Dad have access to these playlists for accountability. No headphones.
- When they are seventeen and a senior in high school, they can listen to whatever they want however they want. But communication is open with Mom and Dad.

TV/Movies
- When they are ten years old, they can watch shows and movies with Mom and Dad or preapproved by Mom and Dad. Mostly G and PG material.
- When they are thirteen, they can watch content a little more mature, but only with Mom and Dad.
- When they are fifteen, they are trusted to start watching some mature content on their own (mature, not profane), but dialoguing with Mom and Dad about what they saw.
- When they are seventeen and a senior in high school, they can choose what they want to watch. But communication is open with Mom and Dad.

Apps and Social Media
- When they are ten years old, they can play with the family iPad, only accessing websites, games, and apps that Mom and Dad have okayed.
- When they are thirteen, they can have their own device, but Mom and Dad use parental settings blocking out (most) inappropriate content, and Mom and Dad are the only ones with the password

and the ability to download new apps.

- When they are fifteen, they are trusted to start navigating some websites, social media, and apps on their own, but Mom and Dad still have the password and can monitor browsing history, etc. Settings are such that apps cannot be deleted—only Mom and Dad can delete (so they see what apps have been accessed).

- When they are seventeen and a senior in high school, they can download and browse whatever they like. But communication is open with Mom and Dad.

I wish I would have implemented this kind of incremental independence from the beginning with all of my kids. Being strict made sense when they were young. But I kept making these kinds of decisions for my son Alec when he was sixteen and seventeen.

Think about this logic for a second. . .or lack thereof. What was my plan?

It's the question I ask parents whenever they ask me, "At what age should I let my kid. . ."

I ask them, "When do you plan to hand them the reins for the first time—when they're in a college dorm by themselves or when they're still under your roof under the safety of your shadow?"

Let's be real. Do you think our eighteen-year-olds are going to call us from their Marine barracks, their college dorm, or their own apartment and ask, "Dad, can I watch *Game of Thrones*?"

If we haven't equipped them to make these decisions by then, we haven't done our job.

WHAT IF THEY AREN'T READY?

Sometimes our seventeen- and eighteen-year-olds aren't ready to be making decisions on their own. In fact, their little sister, who is only fifteen, is making far better choices.

It's hard when our "legal adults" didn't get the memo they are adults, so much so that it's painfully obvious to everyone.

My wife, Lori, helped with the four- and five-year-old class at church recently and had a delightful conversation with a mature little five-year-old girl we'll call Judith. She was extremely observant and verbal for her age. By the time Lori was done spending an hour with her, she knew almost everything about her family.

"We have someone living with us," Judith offered.

"Oh really?" Lori asked. "Why is that?"

"Well, her parents kicked her out of her house," Judith explained, "and now she doesn't have anywhere to live. So she lives with us."

"Well, how old is she?"

"She's nineteen. She sleeps in my room in the top bunk. But she's not a very good roommate."

"Oh really?" Lori asked. "Why not?"

"She doesn't go to bed when she's supposed to. She just stares at her phone."

"Well, sometimes grown-ups can decide for themselves what time to go to bed."

"Oh," Judith interrupted, "she's *not* a grown-up."

"Oh really?" my wife asked, trying not to giggle. "How old do you have to be to be a grown-up?"

Judith thought for a moment and then answered, "I don't know. But she's definitely not a grown-up."

Sometimes our kids are eighteen going on thirteen. Especially boys. Research reveals the male brain often doesn't finish developing until the midtwenties. Until then, there's a lot of "do what feels good at the moment." Blend that kind of cerebral activity with a world full of temporary distractions all screaming, "Do what feels good at the moment!" It can be a recipe for disaster.

The best you can do is consider the big picture. After age eighteen, our kids can move out completely on their own if they want. My son did. He didn't like the rules, so he left to figure out life on his own.

In hindsight, I think I was too strict for too long. I never gave him enough of a chance to be a man. Yes, this is hard when a man is acting like a boy. But consider the alternative. Either you equip him to make decisions and release him to his consequences, or you try to hold on tight only to watch him slowly slip away.

Does this mean we need to let our kids violate "house rules"?

Please don't misunderstand. "No rules" doesn't mean your kids can deal drugs out of the house, come home drunk every Saturday morning, and have their significant other spend the night. It's okay to have house rules—the same types of rules they'll have in the military or on their college campus.

Just don't let those rules turn into "I don't like that song; turn it off!"

We can't parent our kids forever. Take Andy Stanley's advice: *Begin with the end in mind.*

When do you want your kids to be able to make decisions on their own?

What's your game plan to equip them for this day?

DOES INCREMENTAL INDEPENDENCE WORK?

My girls are now away at college but come home and live with us for the summer. So I can truly look back in 20/20 and ask myself, *Did this work?*

Absolutely!

In fact, my only regret is that we weren't proactive with incremental independence earlier. My youngest two are the only ones who really experienced it. And for them, the results were amazing!

When my daughters got to their senior year, we gave them the freedom to hang out with whoever they liked, stay out as long as they liked, do whatever they liked. . .(kind of sounds like a Miley Cyrus song).

Here are some of my observations looking back over the last few years:

- During the early toddler years, my kids didn't notice we were strict. They grew up learning, *If Mom and Dad say it, they mean it!*
- As our kids grew older and began spending time with friends, they noticed some of our guardrails were stricter than those in other families. . .or in the families on the Disney Channel! This awareness caused a little pushback. "But Melanie's mom doesn't make her do that!" Or "Hannah Montana's dad doesn't make her do anything!" That's when we

let them in on our plan to give them more freedom as they earned it, eventually setting them free to make their own decisions by their senior year. This prospect excited them.

- They began referring back to that conversation. "This is one of those areas where I believe I've been proving I make good choices." We tried noticing this progress and rewarding good decision making with more freedom.

- As our kids grew into their teens, we had to be proactive and literally force ourselves to "release the grip" and let them make decisions instead of Mom and Dad making all the decisions for them. "Dad, can I download Rihanna?" "No way! . . . I mean. . .let's take a look at her lyrics and tell me your thoughts."

- By the time my daughters were sixteen and then seventeen, we began letting them make big decisions, like going to a dance or staying the night at a friend's house. We'd tell each of them, "You make the decision; then let's talk about it afterward and see how you think it turned out."

- By the time their senior year arrived, "no rules" really wasn't such a big deal. Each of them had been making most of their own decisions by then anyway. In fact, both of them kept asking us permission to go places. I would always have to remind them, "You can do whatever you think is best. What do you think is best?"

- Discussions with us were no longer about trying to convince us to give them permission—they already had that. Now conversations were about what they were learning from their decisions, good and bad.

Now, even though they're both making decisions on their own, they talk with us frequently about their choices, asking advice. We always try to flavor this advice with, "Well, here are some things you could consider. . . ." We provide them with good information so they can make an informed decision. Sometimes they even ask about our experience in the area, giving us opportunities to tell stories of our successes—and our failures.

YOU GOT THIS

Last Father's Day my church showed a powerful video that featured different dads encouraging their kids through important moments in their lives. A dad held his toddler's hands while she navigated her first steps, murmuring, "You got this."

Another dad cheered as his young son went up to bat for the first time. "You got this!"

As another boy took the stage at his school, ready to give a speech, his dad gave him the thumbs-up from the front row, mouthing those familiar words: "You got this."

A bride paused and took a deep breath as she got ready to the walk down the aisle on her wedding day. Her dad grabbed her hand and whispered, "You got this."

And finally the video showed a nervous twentysomething girl sitting by herself in the foyer of a business office waiting for a job interview. Her name was called. She paused and looked at the empty chair next to her. . .where her dad would have been sitting. Then she stood up and whispered to herself, "I got this."

Isn't that exactly what every parent wants? Confident kids who feel loved, encouraged, and equipped to make it on their own?

Are you preparing them for that moment?

LIVING IT OUT THIS WEEK

QUESTIONS TO DISCUSS WITH YOUR SPOUSE AND/OR OTHER PARENTS

1. What is one thing in this chapter that made you think?
2. Why is it a good idea to have more rules when our kids are young?
3. How do you know when to begin letting your kids have more freedom?
4. What do you think Andy Stanley meant when he told his kids, "We want you to have the same freedom you have your freshman year of college while you are at home with us"?
5. What might this segue look like in your home in regard to bedtime and curfew?
6. What might this segue look like in your home with Netflix and YouTube?
7. What might this segue look like in your home when it comes to apps and social media?
8. What is one thing you read in this chapter that you would like to implement this week? When will you try it?

CHANGE 6

ADD A QUESTION MARK

In 2015, author Alexandra Samuel gathered data from more than ten thousand North American parents about how they handle the issue of "screen time."[1] Her research revealed that parents fall into one of three groups. Each group seems to carry its own distinct attitude toward technology.

The first group she labeled *enablers*. This is by far the largest group. (The McAfee study I referred to earlier revealed 74 percent of parents fall into this category.) These parents have given in to the pressure from their kids and other families around them. They let their kids choose how much media is appropriate.

Samuel called the second group *limiters*. This is the group of parents whose favorite button is the OFF button. Their solution is simply to ban or limit screen time. I meet plenty of these parents in churches where I teach workshops.

The last group isn't swayed by social pressure and doesn't see any benefit to turning off screens their kids will eventually just turn on, figuring, *How will this prepare our kids for a world embracing more and more technology each year?* This group of parents has found the best practice is taking an active role in walking with their kids as they learn about technology and guiding them through it step by step. That's probably why Samuel called this group *mentors*.

Samuel found mentors to be the "most successful in preparing their kids for a world filled with screens." They dialogue with their kids more than twice as much as limiters and are far more likely to research specific devices or programs for their kids (44 percent of mentors do that at least once a week, compared to 31 percent of enablers and 14 percent of limiters).

If you're like me, you're already placing yourself in one of these three categories. I was a limiter—big-time! And if you read my previous chapter about the segue, you felt my frustration as I realized being a limiter proved ineffective with my oldest. The limiter makes all the decisions for his kids, and they never learn to discern for themselves.

Here's what's funny: this struggle isn't anything new.

Sure, smartphones are new, social media is relatively new, selfies are new. . .in fact, some other new fad probably went viral before the ink dried in this book you're holding in your hand (unless you have the eBook—then it was before the pixels arranged themselves).

But the practice of walking alongside our kids through all of these changes?

Not new.

God told us to do that a long time ago. (It's in Deuteronomy 6. We'll look at that passage in depth in the next chapter.) And it's one of the most effective ways to raise kids who become decision makers.

Then how come these "mentor" parents are in the minority?

The answer is painfully clear.

Good parenting takes time and energy.

My friend Paul Kent wrote a Star Wars devotional.[2]
I got a chance to read it before it was published. It was a
creative little book for teenagers, taking elements from the
Star Wars films and applying them to everyday life. In the
introduction to the book, he shared an intriguing story
from his childhood. You see, like me, he was a kid when the
first Star Wars film was first released on May 25, 1977. All
his friends went to see it and immediately started talking
about it every day at school.

I remember the time well. Stores began filling their
shelves with Star Wars toys, puzzles, and pajamas. Kids
wore Star Wars T-shirts to school. They wore Darth Vader
costumes for Halloween. One of my friends even had Star
Wars sheets!

But Paul wasn't allowed to go see Star Wars. His parents held strong to their beliefs that Hollywood was of the
devil!

Paul felt like he was literally the only kid who hadn't
seen the film. But his parents wouldn't budge.

Soon the movie wasn't in theaters anymore, and there
was no renting it or buying it. Back in the '70s, people didn't
have VCRs yet. Paul had missed out.

But hope wasn't lost. (Or should I say, *A New Hope*
wasn't lost?) The film was rereleased in theaters some time
later. Films used to do that if they were a big enough box
office smash. Paul saw this as his opportunity. He asked his
parents again and again until they finally gave in.

This is the part where I burst out laughing: his parents
didn't want to see it, so they just dropped him off at the
theater to watch it by himself.

Let that sink in for a moment.

This is the emblematic response of the "limiter" parent. They start by limiting. "You can't do it!"

But then their kids bother them until the parents can't fight the battle anymore (or they realize that the battle wasn't worth fighting in the first place), so they give in.

Since my friend's parents objected to the film so unwaveringly in the first place, didn't they think it would be smart to at least go watch this film they had deemed unfit for their child? Did an angel come down from heaven in a dream and show these parents that *Star Wars* was now okay? Did Master Yoda make these parents "unlearn what they had learned"?

Why the 180-degree turn?

Even more importantly, don't you think this would be an opportune moment, perhaps a perfect moment, to "co-view" this film with your child and talk about what you saw? Your boy has been begging you to watch this film for over a year. You've got this kid in the palm of your hand. You could probably convince him to read the entire book of Psalms with you at breakfast each morning for a month in exchange for watching this film.

And yet you just drop him off at the curb?

Hilarious!

Parents! Hear me! This is your chance. You can make an incredible difference in the life of your kids when you heed God's advice and walk through life with them, dialoguing about what God has done for them.

Most parents would love to engage in meaningful conversations with their kids, talking about stuff that matters, but don't know the secret to accomplishing this pattern of teaching.

Do you know how to be a mentor parent, instead of a limiter or an enabler?

The secret is in the punctuation.

We need to learn to use the question mark.

THE QUESTION MARK

The best way to teach our kids is to rephrase our teaching and add a question mark. Don't get me wrong. I'm not simply repeating what I said in "Change 3: Notice" when I encouraged you to use questions to get to know your kids better. As much as that is an excellent practice, I'm now suggesting you use questions for something different.

Teach with questions!

Stop telling your kids what *to do*; instead, ask them what they *should do*.

I was terrible at this. My go-to response was lecturing. If you asked my kids, they'd tell you, "Dad loved to lecture." Sadly, it took me quite a while to realize lecturing isn't half as effective as asking a question and listening.

So I made a change. I began using questions to teach. This practice moved me from lecturing to listening.

Apparently I'm not alone. As I asked other parents to look back at their own parenting, numerous parents cited listening as a skill they wish they had mastered. Like this mother of two boys now in college:

> *One of the things I would do over would be to ask more questions and be a better listener.*

*More times than I'd like to admit, I gave them
the answer or told our sons what they "should
do." Some of life's most valuable lessons come
from figuring them out on our own.*

So what does this look like?

Your son asks you, "Can I hold off on my homework and go play football with Jake?"

Instead of answering yes or no, ask him, "Should you?" Or "What do you think is wise?"

Jesus did this all the time! He had an amazing way of using questions to teach people truth. Consider how shrewd this strategy is. When Jesus came upon a teaching moment, He often opted for asking a question and listening instead of lecturing. The result was powerful.

If we look at the Gospel record, we'll discover Jesus asking literally hundreds of questions. Let's take a quick peek at just a few of the questions He asked:

1. "Do you believe that I am able to do this?" (Matthew 9:28)
2. "Who do people say the Son of Man is?" (Matthew 16:13)
3. "Who do you say I am?" (Matthew 16:15)
4. "What good will it be for someone to gain the whole world, yet forfeit their soul?" (Matthew 16:26)
5. "Can you drink the cup I am going to drink?" (Matthew 20:22)
6. "What do you think about the Messiah? Whose son is he?" (Matthew 22:42)

7. "How will you escape being condemned to hell?" (Matthew 23:33)
8. "Why are you thinking these things?" (Mark 2:8)
9. "When I broke the five loaves for the five thousand, how many basketfuls of pieces did you pick up?" (Mark 8:19)
10. "What did Moses command you?" (Mark 10:3)
11. "Why do you call me good?" (Mark 10:18)
12. "Why are you thinking these things in your hearts?" (Luke 5:22)
13. "What is written in the Law? How do you read it?" (Luke 10:26)
14. "Why are you troubled, and why do doubts rise in your minds?" (Luke 24:38)
15. "I have spoken to you of earthly things and you do not believe; how then will you believe if I speak of heavenly things?" (John 3:12)
16. "Do you want to get well?" (John 5:6)
17. "Where are they? Has no one condemned you?" (John 8:10)
18. "Do you believe this?" (John 11:26)
19. "Do you understand what I have done for you?" (John 13:12)
20. "Do you love me?" (John 21:17)

This list accounts for less than 10 percent of Jesus' questions found in the Gospels. Jesus asked a lot of questions!

I love how Jesus used questions to provoke people to think. For example, in Matthew 16, when He asked His disciples, "Who do people say the Son of Man is?" (verse 13), this wasn't a probing question. Jesus was just asking what the crowds thought. But then Jesus made it more personal by asking, "Who do *you* say I am?" (verse 15, emphasis added).

We can learn quite a bit from Jesus' approach. Start general, then get more personal. In other words, don't scare them away with the first question.

Think what this might look like with your kids: "Do you ever get irritated when you're trying to hang out with your friends and they're staring at their phones the whole time?" *Pause to hear their answer.* "Do you ever do that with your friends?"

Jesus used this kind of questioning to make a point. We can do the same.

LEAD THEM TO THE DECISION

Teachers use this method constantly. Asking students questions requires them to process the information they have just heard and use it to discover an answer.

My mother was an English professor at California State University in Sacramento, and she used this method on me growing up. I hated it! Whenever I had a question about the composition of a paper I was writing, she would never spell out an answer for me. I would ask, "What should I write in this paragraph?" She would always respond, "Well, what do you think you should put there?"

I'd always balk. "Come on, Mom! Just tell me the answer!"

Young people don't always like it when we ask them to think. Sure, it's nice that we aren't telling them what to do. They enjoy being treated like an adult who can make decisions. But at times my kids probably would have just preferred I gave them an answer.

"Dad, can I watch the new Will Ferrell movie?"

"I don't know. Would you let your kid watch it?"

Sigh!

They wouldn't mind if I just said yes. But they don't necessarily want every decision to become a huge discussion about the behaviors and attitudes young people glean from entertainment media.

You might be tempted to give in and answer for them. What good would that do them? (See what I did there? I asked you a question.)

It's your job as a parent to make them think through decisions. Remember the old adage, "You can lead a horse to water, but you can't make them drink." The same is true with today's young people. It's your job as a parent to lead them to the right decision. But they are the ones who need to learn to make said decision.

Sometimes the questions don't have to turn into huge discussions. Do your best to just make your kids think.

"Dad, can I go to the drive-in this Friday?"

"I don't know much about your plans. You tell me if you should go."

This principle of teaching with questions doesn't mean you let your kids make every choice. When my girls were in middle school, I used this same method, and then I still reserved the right to make the final decision (because they were still young). So if my daughter Ashley approached me and asked if she could download a certain song onto her playlist, I would start by asking, "What do you think of the song's lyrics?" After discussing it, if she still wanted it, but I disagreed, I would tell her, "Sorry, Ashley. I just don't think twelve-year-olds need to be listening to songs about midnight booty calls." Interestingly enough, it rarely came to that with Ashley. Most of the time she was making good choices.

There's one catch to using this method of leading our kids to decisions: we need to actually know where we're leading them!

That means we need to know what values we stand for and what hills we die on. Sometimes we moms and dads need to talk and come to agreement about where we'll lead our kids. If Mom lets little Christina watch anything she wants, and Dad doesn't, Christina is never going to ask Dad (today's kids are savvy like that). So do your best to talk about these bigger decisions and come to an agreement as parents. It's okay to delay your kids and tell them honestly, "As you're weighing whether downloading this app is a good decision, your father and I will look into it as well and see what's best. Let's talk tomorrow and see what all three of us think."

Yes, this is much more difficult in split homes. When your kids are living in two homes with two different sets of values, often the rules will look different in each setting. In this situation, do your best to try to come to agreement between parents. But if the other parent wants to do things their own way, it might be a tough battle to fight. The best you can do is remember the influence you can have while bonding with your kids when you have them and providing realistic boundaries in your home. The biggest impact you'll make in this situation is through your own attitudes and behaviors. If your kids see you living a life of love, grace, and purity, then it will be hard to argue with a life so well lived.

Know where *you* are leading your kids.

In my house, this process is much easier when my wife and I are spending time reading our Bibles together. The Bible is our source of wisdom, and when the two of us are reading it together and dialoguing about what we read, God's teaching becomes cemented into our lives so we know what the truth looks like, especially in a world so full of cunning lies. (More on this in the next chapter.)

ON THE FLY

So what does teaching with questions look like day to day? How can we replace "You should" with "Should you?"

Let's be real. These difficult parenting scenarios have a way of sneaking up on us when we're unprepared. Our kids will run up to us while we're in the middle of something important (almost strategically) and quickly ask, "Can I go to Michael's house and watch the new TV show with Dwayne 'The Rock' Johnson? It's about football. Michael's mom lets him watch it. Please!"

Now we have to make a decision on the fly. And it's difficult to make wise decisions in five seconds or less. *The Rock? He's done kids' movies. It's probably clean, right?*

Here are some thoughts to consider:

1. *Remember to phrase your answer as a question.* If you are pretty sure you need to tell your son no, don't just say no; lead him to the no. So in this example, maybe say, "What do you think you should do?" If

he replies, "I think I should watch it!" then try my next idea.

2. *Offer to watch it together.* Often our kids know a lot more about what they're asking than they lead us to believe. That's where the advice of the American Academy of Pediatrics to "co-view" comes in handy. Watch it with them. Or in this situation, instead of just saying no, ask them, "Should we watch it together as a family tonight and see what we all think?" If your kids still say yes, then consider the next idea.

3. *Delay.* If your kids are still young and you don't have enough information. . .delay! Don't be afraid to say, "I can't make that decision right now because I don't have enough information. The answer isn't *no*; it's *not now*. But I'm happy to look up the show or maybe even try the show with you later and see what you think."

5. *Remember incremental independence.* If your kids are twelve, then they still need a lot of guidance, so don't be afraid to veto their decision. But if they're seventeen years old and in their senior year, after asking them what they think is best, release them to their decision. Let them fail if necessary. Then be there to lovingly pick them up. Maybe offer, "Well, as you know, you can make this decision on your own. So make the choice and let's grab Starbucks tomorrow and you can tell me what you thought."

Make sure that Starbucks time isn't filled with lectures or "I told you so." Use questions to lead them to the truth.

Another helpful tool for thinking on the fly is a handful of versatile questions you can use and adapt in a variety of settings with your kids.

Here are some of my favorites:

- *"Was he right?"* I've used this question with my kids probably more than any other question. If my kids tell me about something questionable their friend did at school, or if they show me a music video on YouTube where a guy is hooking up with girls, instead of lecturing I just ask, "Was he right?"
- *"How do you think he will feel about that decision next week/month/year?"* This is a good question prompting young people to think beyond the temporary thrill of the moment and to consider long-term ramifications. Kind of like when Dr. Phil asks, "How's that working out for you?"
- *"How do you think he got to this point?"* This gets your kids to ponder the choices someone made leading to the situation at hand.
- *"Give me two or three alternate ways this situation could have been handled."* This question helps them think through options. Kids should understand they always have several choices how to respond, and each choice has consequences good or bad. That's why you follow that question up with. . .

- *"Knowing what you know now, which one would you have chosen? Which one would you as a parent choose?"* This helps them consider positive alternatives.
- *"What does the Bible say about this?"* This question helps them go to the source of true wisdom.
- *"Why do you think this is so?"* If you ever see a truth manifested clearly through a story, simply ask this question so your kids can explain why. This is a great question when you see statistics showing consequences of behaviors.

You can use these types of questions over family dinner. You can use them when you're watching the news or reading the paper. You can use them if you're reading the Bible together as a family.

Try it next time you see an article like this one entitled "Sexual Media Exposure, Sexual Behavior, and Sexual Violence Victimization in Adolescence." Here's just a snippet of this scholarly study:

> *The relative odds of ever having sex were almost 4 times higher for youth who reported some of at least one media they consumed, and more than 5 times higher for youth who reported that many or almost all/all of at least one media they consumed depicted sexual situations, compared to youth who reported that almost none/none of the media they consumed depicted sexual situations.*[3]

Rephrase it or explain it quickly if you must; then ask: "Why do you think this is so?"

Imagine the discussion this one question could incite. (And if you read more of the report, you'll find it provides much more data provoking conversation.)

The key to this whole approach of teaching with questions is to limit lecturing while cultivating listening. Fight the temptation to sit them down and set them straight. Let questions guide them to the answer.

"Should you?"

This approach takes time and energy. That's why most parents don't do it. They either enforce a bunch of limitations with no conversations. . .or they let their kids do whatever they want. Either way is much easier than walking along the road with our kids and leading them toward the truth.

Let's dive into the next chapter and talk a little more about that.

LIVING IT OUT THIS WEEK

QUESTIONS TO DISCUSS WITH YOUR SPOUSE AND/OR OTHER PARENTS

1. What is one thing in this chapter that stood out to you?
2. Which of the three types of parents—enablers, limiters, mentors—do you think you identified with the most?
3. How's that working out for you?
4. How do questions help parents become "mentor parents" instead of limiters or enablers?
5. Why do you think Jesus used so many questions?
6. Can you think of an example of you using questions to lead any of your kids to a decision? How did it work?
7. Can you think of a time when you should have used this method but didn't? How would you handle it if you had a do-over?
8. How would asking, "Should we watch it together?" help you in some of these "on the fly" situations?
9. Where can you see yourself using a versatile question like "Is he right?" or "Why do you think this is so?"
10. What is one thing you read in this chapter that you would like to implement this week? When will you try it?

CHANGE 7

WALK WITH

"What is the best way to pass on values to our kids?"

It's one of the most common questions I hear from parents after my workshops. The question comes in many different forms.

"How can we help our kids establish a faith of their own?"

"What are the best ways to mentor our kids and teach them truth?"

"How can I teach my kids values in a world that doesn't seem to have any?"

Truth is an interesting term. The word is probably on the endangered species list, at least with the definition we once knew. Today's young people aren't very concerned about "truth"; they're more interested in what works for them.

I guess we shouldn't be surprised, in a world where almost every three-year-old in America can sing every word to the Disney song "Let It Go," which moralizes testing limits, no right, no wrong, no rules. . .concepts that make you wonder how much of this our kids are grasping as they belt out those very words.

Don't worry. I'm not turning fanatical on you. I'm not going to ask you to stop using a certain hairspray because the company supports a cause I don't agree with. I simply want us to pause and think about what our kids are swallowing from this culture hook, line, and sinker. We're raising a generation of kids who are learning to make decisions based on a moral code of "what's right for me."

Research reveals three-quarters of Millennials (74 percent) agree with the statement "Whatever is right for your life or works best for you is the only truth you can know," compared to only 38 percent of the generation of Elders.[1]

How's that for a rapid change in morality over generations?

Please understand. This isn't meant as a criticism of "today's kids." It's actually a criticism of us—the adults who have raised them this way. One way or another we have allowed our kids to adopt a very convenient morality: *Do what feels right in the moment. Go with your gut. No one can tell you what's right for you.*

And how do you think this will work out for most?

How do family, moral, or even biblical values fit into this kind of worldview?

What will this kind of morality look like day to day?

For most young people it means adopting the moral code of the majority. In other words:

- If everyone else sleeps with someone on the second date, that's the standard.
- If everyone else says a little bit of drugs can't hurt anyone, then why not?
- If a lie will get you out of trouble, then don't hesitate.
- Truth or character doesn't matter.
- Living for the moment is what matters.

I saw this mode of thinking played out to the extreme when my wife and I counseled a nineteen-year-old girl who was having a tough time staying in school or keeping a job. This Millennial had been raised in a good home, gone to church her entire life, and even served as a student leader in her youth ministry, going on mission trips and serving the poor. Once in college, she started drinking, stopped going to class, and eventually became more interested in partying than finishing anything she started.

Her aunt took her in and gave her very few rules: *Work or go to school, don't come home drunk, and don't have anyone over while we're away.* The young girl didn't keep *any* of these rules. Not one.

Lori and I chatted with this young lady one afternoon after she got caught having a party at her aunt's house when she was away. She defended herself. "Her rules are impossible."

"Well," I offered, "when you violate the trust of the people who love you, you're not only hurting your relationship with them; you're possibly evicting yourself from the only place in town with free room and board."

She dug her feet in and argued, "They just don't understand. . . ."

Her moral code was all about *her* at the expense of everyone around her.

Sadly, this young woman's philosophy of "do whatever works for you" was slowly catching up with her. The consequences of her bad behaviors were now enslaving her. She was jobless, homeless, and friendless. Selfishness has its drawbacks. Truth has a way of revealing itself. . .eventually.

So let me ask the question again: How can we raise moral kids in an immoral world?

The youth ministry world has been asking a similar question over the last decade: How can we develop a faith in young people that lasts beyond high school?

It's the question youth leaders have been wrestling with for years having watched countless young people walk away from their faith after high school. In reality, many of them exit the church way before that. Look at any church youth group. Upperclassmen are the minority. Sure, jobs and college apps demand a lot from juniors and seniors, but does that account for such a drastic decrease?

I speak to young people at churches, camps, and conferences across the world, and I see the same thing almost everywhere I go. The older teens get, the less likely you'll find them in church.

What happened?

What made these kids lose interest in the very faith they were raised believing?

Guess what—this isn't anything new. In fact, this is an old problem. A four-thousand-year-old problem to be exact.

In Deuteronomy 6, Moses has an important talk with God's people (I told you we would dive into this passage). As he addressed them, he pleaded with them not to forget all God had done for them. He specifically asked them to commit wholeheartedly to God's commands (verse 6).

But he didn't stop there:

> *Impress them on your children. Talk about them when you sit at home and when you walk along*

the road, when you lie down and when you
get up. Tie them as symbols on your hands and
bind them on your foreheads. Write them on the
doorframes of your houses and on your gates.
(verses 7–9)

Let's be honest. This is a tough Bible passage for most of us to take seriously. Think about it. This instruction goes way beyond just dragging our kids to a Sunday church service. It requires more than just dropping our kids off at youth group once a week!

Moses tells these parents to talk with their kids about God's story while sitting at home, walking along the road, getting up, and lying down. In fact, he asks us to follow this instruction in everything we do (the true ramifications of his "tie them as symbols on your hands") and in everything we think about ("bind them on your foreheads"). That might make us think twice about some of the TV we watch.

Moses basically warned God's people, "Don't let your kids forget what the Lord has done for you!" He even spelled out what this might look like for most families day to day (and they weren't even distracted by their mobile devices back then).

The question is, did they do it?

Sadly, if you flip ahead in your Bible just a few books, you'll find the answer in the book of Judges. That generation of parents died off and the generation of kids grew up: "After that generation died, another generation grew up who did not acknowledge the Lord or remember the mighty things he had done for Israel" (2:10 NLT).

They didn't remember what God had done for them. They didn't come to faith on their own.

Why?

The parents didn't commit wholeheartedly to God's commands and impress them on their children at home, walking along the road, getting up in the morning, and going to bed at night. . . .

And four thousand years later, God's people are the same.

Is this the kind of legacy you want to leave?

How can we avoid this tragic forfeiture of our call as parents?

WALKING WITH

The solution lies in the "walking with."

It's the Christmas message when you think about it. God came down and became man. Jesus is God incarnate. We sing about it every December. His name is Emmanuel, which means what?

God is *with* us.

Not. . .God is in the other room watching TV.

God is *with* us.

Jesus lived this out while He was on earth. He didn't sit on a pedestal somewhere; He walked elbow to elbow *with* the people, sitting with them, talking with them, eating with them, touching them, and interacting in real life. The more people hung out with Him, the more they gleaned from Him because He actually took the time to notice them and meet their needs.

Jesus even selected a group of twelve disciples who

would carry on His ministry after He left. He didn't sit these guys down in a classroom and make them study. He walked with them for three years, teaching them as He went.

He walked *with* them.

The more I research parenting, the more I hear experts communicate the effectiveness of walking *with* our kids. (Remember the "mentor parents" in the previous chapter?) Not posting a list of rules. Not releasing them to do whatever they want. Walking with them.

The more I ask parents about their successes and failures, the more they express the effectiveness of walking *with* their kids. And the more I look back on my own parenting, the more I realize that the impact of what I *said to* them was miniscule in comparison to what I *did with* them.

With is always far more effective than *to*.

If I had to do it all over again, I'd focus on the *with*.

So how can we live this out? How can we walk with our kids?

I don't have a secret recipe, and I don't have a few simple tasks we can check off each day. What I can offer are three noteworthy observations about what "walking with" actually looks like in the world today. Hopefully these insights will give you ideas for steps you can take in your life, with your family, in your home.

1. "Walking with" Begins with Our Faith

Passing on a legacy of faith begins with our own faith.

I wish I could give you a shortcut, but I can't. The fact is, your faith in action is the best teaching tool you'll ever use. On one hand, this is very daunting, because all of us are imperfect. We think, *I'm so messed up, my kids are sure to be messed up.* That's where God's grace comes in. If you surrender to God and give Him permission to work in your life, He'll give you a fresh start. Your kids will notice this transformation, and it will give them hope. They, like you, will see that God can take something imperfect and begin changing it for the better.

On the other hand, your faith in action makes your job of walking with your kids on this journey waaaay easier, because your kids will learn much more from your actions than your words. This journey is so much more about leaving a legacy of love and connection than teaching principles.

What did this look like in my life?

You've heard me confess many of my mess-ups in this book, from my temper to my shortsightedness. If I may, allow me to share a couple of areas where God worked through me.

My kids heard me say, "Don't lie. Always keep your word." But they truly learned the principle when our family kept commitments, time and time again, even when they weren't fun commitments.

"Why do we have to go?"

"Because we told them we'd be there. And if we tell someone we'll be there, then we'll be there. They'll know they can always count on us."

My kids heard me say, "Love your neighbor." But the words truly made an impact when they saw us stocking our car with McDonald's gift cards and bottles of water so we could give them to homeless people on the side of the road every time we encountered them, when we tipped restaurant servers extra well, when we brought meals to people in need.

Our actions spoke louder than words every time.

You can teach what you know, but you can only reproduce who you truly are.

As you walk with your kids on this journey, you'll notice the road is littered with distractions, which is why we need to teach our kids how to navigate obstacles.

2. *"Walking with" Means Teaching Navigation Skills*

The world has always offered numerous alluring rabbit trails diverting us from the wise path. Today these distractions are even more abundant because the device in our pocket provides us with anything and everything. That's why it's even more essential for today's parents to walk *with* their kids and teach them to navigate around these enticements.

I've highlighted some of these influences in past chapters, even giving you a few hints about navigating the world of social media and technology with your kids. I promised you more, so let's get even more specific and look at some examples of ways parents can teach their kids to steer away from these distractions.

Notice I didn't say parents should do the steering for their kids.

We need to teach our kids how to steer, incrementally allowing them more opportunities to do their own navigating as they approach independence.

What does this actually look like?

It doesn't mean becoming a "drill sergeant" parent obsessed with boundaries; it simply means providing helpful guardrails to keep our kids on course.

Let me point to the recommendations of two experts. The first comes from *Pediatrics*, the journal of the American Academy of Pediatrics (AAP). Here are just a few guidelines put forth in the article for today's families:

- Limit the amount of total entertainment screen time to less than one to two hours per day.
- Keep the TV set and Internet-connected electronic devices out of the child's bedroom.
- Monitor the media children are using and accessing, including any websites they are visiting and social media sites they may be using.
- Co-view TV shows, movies, and videos with children and teenagers, and use this practice as a way of discussing important family values.
- Model active parenting by establishing a family home use plan for all media. As part of the plan, enforce a mealtime and bedtime "curfew" for media devices, including cell phones. Establish reasonable but firm rules about cell phones, texting, Internet, and social media use.[2]

The AAP isn't alone in its recommendations to parents. Common Sense Media provides "smart strategies" for managing your kids' media and technology. These strategies include the following:

- Check out your kids' social sites. Literally ask them to show you where they visit, what they do there, who they talk to, and what they upload.
- Watch them play their favorite games or even play with them.
- Share music. Play music with them and ask them to play you their favorite songs. Take advantage of safety mode features on sites like YouTube where parents can block inappropriate content.
- Take control of your TV. Preview shows, and use the remote to avoid bad content.
- Research your kids' apps. Try out the app with your kids.
- Establish a digital code of conduct. Set rules around responsible, respectful usage.[3]

You might have noticed words like *research*, *check out*, and *monitor*. This means we need to take the time to notice where our kids are spending their time. But both of these experts also used words like *play*, *watch*, and *try out*. This means that much of the "noticing" these experts recommend is done in the form of participating in the entertainment media with our kids, watching shows with them, playing games with them, or browsing the apps they enjoy. The more we take part in their lives, the more opportunities we will have to teach good decision making and pass on our family values.

Note what both of these experts did *not* tell you to do. They did *not* say:

- Just get some porn-blocking software, and then you won't ever have to monitor your kids again.
- Just unplug all the devices, move to Amish Pennsylvania, and teach your kids how to churn butter.
- Just ban all entertainment media until they leave the house; then they can figure it out on their own.

As you can see, parenting is a healthy balance of both bonding and boundaries. The more we notice our kids and make efforts to truly get to know them, the more we'll know what boundaries are actually helpful and, more importantly, the more we'll be able to engage in meaningful conversation about the stuff that matters.

It's pretty cool to see the journal our family pediatrician reads recommending that families play together, watch media together, and talk about important family values. . .which brings me to my last observation.

3. It All Comes Down to Love

So what is the most important value we need to pass on? That's a huge question.

What should our conversations be sure to include while we're sitting at home, walking along the road, getting up, and lying down?

What is most important?

Sadly, Christians haven't always aligned themselves with biblical teaching when answering this question. Historically, Christians have done some stupid things "in Jesus' name." People have spewed venomous words and hate, supposedly in defense of Christian principles. . .all while missing the biggest Christian principle.

What is this principle I'm talking about?

It's hard to miss if you pick up your Bible and read it. It even uses words like "the most important thing" when it talks about it.

Love.

Love is the most important thing.

It's all throughout there. Like when the people of Galatia were being misled by a bunch of religious guys who were trying to convince them they needed to adhere to certain rules and practices to be accepted by God. The apostle Paul corrected them and told them that only a true faith in Jesus saved them, not rules. Then he said this: "What is important is faith expressing itself in love" (Galatians 5:6 NLT).

But Paul knew his readers would probably miss this. So he went into even more detail, warning his people against false teachers and pleading that they live out their faith by serving one another in love. Then he said this: "For the whole law can be summed up in this one command: 'Love your neighbor as yourself'" (Galatians 5:14 NLT).

There it is again. It's all throughout the Bible. Even in the Old Testament: "I want you to show love, not offer sacrifices" (Hosea 6:6 NLT).

It's all through the Gospel accounts. Like when the Pharisees were quizzing Jesus and asked Him what was most important:

> *"Teacher, which is the most important commandment in the law of Moses?"*
> *Jesus replied, " 'You must love the LORD*

your God with all your heart, all your soul,
and all your mind.' This is the first and greatest
commandment. A second is equally important:
'Love your neighbor as yourself.' The entire law
and all the demands of the prophets are based
on these two commandments." (Matthew
22:36–40 NLT)

Or how about the famous "love chapter" that is read at almost every wedding, the passage that literally starts with Paul saying, "If I had the gift of prophecy, and if I understood all of God's secret plans and possessed all knowledge, and if I had such faith that I could move mountains, but didn't love others, I would be nothing" (1 Corinthians 13:2 NLT).

Or from the pen of Peter: "Most important of all, continue to show deep love for each other, for love covers a multitude of sins" (1 Peter 4:8 NLT).

Wow! That's good to know, Peter, because I've got plenty of sins!

Love keeps coming up again and again as most important. How is it that Christians miss this?

More specifically, if we aren't teaching our kids love, what are we teaching our kids?

The chief complaint of nonbelievers is that Christians are hateful and hypocritical. Don't worry, I'm not going to start defending nonbelievers or try to convince you to change sides on issues. I'm just going to ask you, How did believers get this reputation? Why is it that even Gandhi said, "I like your Christ; I do not like your Christians. Your Christians are so unlike your Christ"?[4]

Perhaps we need to start teaching our kids that love is the most important thing. Or better yet, as I mentioned just a few pages ago, maybe we need to start modeling this truth so our kids learn it as they're walking with us.

How can we do this?

- Attend a church where Jesus' teachings are taught and love is lived out.
- Look for opportunities to serve in your community, and let God's love work through you, giving glory to God, not yourself.
- Be a light in your everyday activities on your own street and in your own neighborhood so others will see your love and maybe even ask you about the source of that love. (1 Peter 3:15–16)
- Take your kids through the Gospels so they can learn Jesus' teachings firsthand and see how He responded in love to sinners without bending His morality in the process.
- Remember the biblical mandate of love in every decision you make for your family.
- When you mess up (and you will), ask for forgiveness and demonstrate that the relationship is what's important.

Imagine if all of God's people were loving others proactively like this. What would this look like in your home?

WITH

Your kids don't need parents who let them do whatever they want.

Your kids don't need parents who just set a bunch of rules.

Your kids need parents who will *walk with* them, equipping them for that day when they have to make decisions on their own.

Are you equipping them for that day?

LIVING IT OUT THIS WEEK

QUESTIONS TO DISCUSS WITH YOUR SPOUSE AND/OR OTHER PARENTS

1. What is one thing in this chapter that made you think?
2. Why do you think the overwhelming majority of twentysomethings believe, "Whatever is right for your life or works best for you is the only truth you can know," compared to only one-third of their grandparents?
3. How can we live out Moses' command to talk with our kids while sitting at home, walking along the road, getting up, and lying down (Deuteronomy 6:6–9)?
4. Why do you think an entire generation of God's people fell away from following God (Judges 2:10)? What would that look like now?
5. What are some ways Jesus modeled "walking with" us?
6. What are some ways today's parents can stay informed about their kids' use of social media and entertainment using the "walking with" method?
7. How can you approach "co-viewing" some of this content with your kids?
8. What is a specific way you can model love in your home or community?
9. What is one thing you read in this chapter that you would like to implement this week? When will you try it?

WHAT NOW?

25 WAYS TO APPLY WHAT YOU'VE JUST READ

I don't know about you, but I've read plenty of good books and articles, thinking, *This is phenomenal stuff!* but then never really took action to apply what I read.

What a tragedy!

You have just read eye-opening research along with the testimony of parents who have looked back at their own parenting in 20/20 and testified, "I wish I would have done this differently!" If you're like me, you're going to make every effort to implement what you've learned. This kind of knowledge is precious!

So how do we put feet to all the pragmatic advice woven throughout this book?

In this short chapter I'm going to keep it simple. Here are twenty-five practical ideas for integrating some of this advice into your parenting practices.

25 WAYS TO WALK WITH YOUR KIDS ON THE ROAD TO ADULTHOOD

1. BREAK FREE

Don't let your past mistakes haunt you. If you've hurt your family in one way or another, humble yourself before them and your God and ask for forgiveness.

2. IDENTIFY CONNECTION VENUES

What are the settings where your kids seem to open up almost instinctively? Be proactive about creating these "connection venues" where conversation happens. For more ideas, read my book *52 Ways to Connect with Your Smartphone Obsessed Kid*.[1]

3. MAKE FAMILY DINNERS A PRIORITY

Try your best to have family dinners as often as possible. Don't worry if you don't have deep conversations every time. Remember, it takes quantity time to achieve those quality-time moments.

4. SHARE HIGHS AND LOWS

If you have trouble kindling conversation at dinner, try asking everyone to share the high and low of their day. A simple practice like this gives everyone a chance to be heard.

5. TRY BURSTS OF "NO TECH"

Start with a "no tech at the table" policy. That means Mom and Dad as well. Then try a "No Tech Tuesday." It's amazing what kinds of conversations can take place when devices are put away.

6. JUST SAY YES

When your kids ask you to do anything that involves connecting with them. . .just say yes! Playing Barbies, building with Legos, taking them shopping to buy supplies for a school project—these are all great opportunities to bond with them.

7. TRY A BOUNDARY FAST

Even if you don't struggle to find bonding time with your kids, try a boundary fast one day. This means you can't correct them or ask them anything that resembles "checking up on them." No boundaries at all. Only bonding. Try it. The house probably won't burn down.

8. WALK AWAY

One of the hardest steps in not getting "caught up in the crazy" is the simple practice of pressing pause and walking away. Give it a try.

9. SEEK TO UNDERSTAND

If your kids engage in an argument with you, don't allow yourself to talk until you ask them at least five questions, hearing their side of the story. Pretend you are their defense attorney preparing their case. Seek to understand what your kids are thinking and feeling.

10. BE A FLY ON THE WALL

Find times to go watch your kids in their element somewhere. Don't spy; just show up, watch, and listen. Young people aren't half as stealthy as they think they are. You can learn a ton just by sitting and watching your kids and their friends.

11. ASK QUESTIONS BASED ON YOUR OBSERVATIONS

Make your bonding time with your kids more about them than you. Ask them questions—not to dig up dirt on them, but to truly get to know them better.

12. DATE YOUR KIDS

Take your kids on dates to places they like. Then actively listen to them like you would someone you were dating. Find out everything you can about them through this process of discovery.

13. JUST SAY NO

What is something that is interfering with your family time? It might not be something bad, but it's taking priority over your kids. Say no for a season and see if that creates opportunities to connect with your kids.

14. BEGIN WITH THE END IN MIND

As your kids approach adolescence, map out the journey to adulthood. Decide what you want to teach your kids by the time they leave the house, and figure out what that journey looks like. How can you begin the segue from high guidance to low guidance?

15. SHOW YOUR KIDS THE MAP

Sit your kids down and share the big picture, explaining why you'll be more strict while they're young, and your goal for them to have no rules their senior year.

16. BECOME DEVICE SAVVY

Begin educating yourself about the apps, games, websites, and shows your kids enjoy. Subscribe to helpful blogs and articles from experts like Common Sense Media and TheSource4Parents.com to stay current.

17. CO-VIEW

Ask your kids to show you some of their favorite apps, games, and shows. Try not to overreact if you see something disturbing. Press pause on your response, and tell them you need to think about what you've seen.

18. ESTABLISH REALISTIC GUARDRAILS

Set some helpful guardrails to keep your kids on course, giving more freedom as they grow. Consider rules about when devices get turned off and what kind of online behaviors are acceptable. Talk about these rules with your kids, and make sure they understand why they exist.

19. ANSWER QUESTIONS WITH QUESTIONS

When your kids ask you permission to do something, try answering their question with a question to help them think through their decision. Ask, "What do you think you should do?" Don't always decide for them.

20. MAXIMIZE TEACHING MOMENTS

If you see a teaching moment, don't make the mistake of lecturing instead of listening. Simply ask questions like "Were they right? How do you think they'll feel about that decision next year? How else could they have handled the situation? What do you think you'd do now that you've had time to think it over?"

21. LOOK FOR OPPORTUNITIES TO SERVE AS A FAMILY

Contact a local food bank or homeless shelter and find an opportunity to serve as a family. Some of these opportunities will arise on your own street. Help an elderly neighbor take care of their yard, shovel snow off their driveway, bring them cookies.

22. TEACH THE TEACHINGS OF JESUS

Read through some of the Gospels so your kids can hear the teachings of Jesus firsthand. Start with Luke; then read John. Then read Acts for a picture of what happened after Jesus' ascension.

23. MENTOR ONE-ON-ONE

When your kids are young, start the habit of meeting with them weekly in a mentoring role. Dads, take your adolescent boys through my book *The Guy's Guide to God, Girls, and the Phone in Your Pocket*.[2] Take your sons or daughters through my book *Sex Matters*.[3]

24. ATTEND A PARENTING WORKSHOP

Look for any opportunity to learn more about parenting. Attend workshops that educate you about youth culture and give you practical tools to help you connect with your kids. Organizations like TheSource4Parents.com and HomeWord.com bring parenting workshops to cities around the world.

25. DIALOGUE WITH OTHER PARENTS

Engage in conversations with other parents about parenting, sharing your successes and failures (keep it about you, respecting your kids' privacy). Use small-group questions like the ones at the end of each chapter of this book to provoke discussion.

NOTES

CHANGE 1: TIP THE SCALES

1. http://www.nielsen.com/content/dam/corporate/us/en/reports-downloads/2016-reports/q4-2015-total-audience-report.pdf, 16.
2. Brigid Schulte, "Making Time for Kids? Study Says Quality Trumps Quantity," *Washington Post*, March 28, 2015, www.washingtonpost.com/local/making-time-for-kids-study-says-quality-trumps-quantity/2015/03/28/10813192-d378-11e4-8fce-3941fc548f1c_story.html.
3. Ibid.
4. The National Center on Addiction and Substance Abuse at Columbia University, *The Importance of Family Dinners VIII*, September 2012, www.centeronaddiction.org/addiction-research/reports/importance-of-family-dinners-2012.

CHANGE 2: LET IT GO

1. http://www.parenting.com/article/how-to-choose-your-battles-1000072888.
2. Stephen R. Covey, *The Seven Habits of Highly Effective People* (New York: Free Press, 1989), www.stephencovey.com/7habits/7habits-habit5.php.
3. Francis of Assisi, "Make Me an Instrument of Your Peace," www.catholic.org/prayers/prayer.php?p=134.

CHANGE 3: NOTICE

1. Sue Klebold, interview with Diane Sawyer, "Silence Broken: A Mother's Reckoning: A Diane Sawyer Special," *20/20*, ABC, February 12, 2016, http://abcnews.go.com/US/fullpage/diane-sawyer-exclusive-sue-klebold-36867525.

2. Jessica Contrera, "13, Right Now," *Washington Post*, May 25, 2016, www.washingtonpost.com/sf/style/wp/2016/05/25/2016/05/25/13-right-now-this-is-what-its-like-to-grow-up-in-the-age-of-likes-lols-and-longing/.

3. Nina Godlewski, "If You Have over 25 Photos on Instagram, You're No Longer Cool," *Tech Insider*, May 26, 2016, www.techinsider.io/teens-curate-their-instagram-accounts-2016-5.

4. Shaunti Feldhahn, "2 Things to Do If You Want Your Teen to Talk to You," *Shaunti Feldhahn: Research, Insight, Hope*, June 29, 2016, www.shaunti.com/2016/06/2-things-to-do-if-you-want-your-teen-to-talk-to-you/.

5. Jonathan McKee, *More Than Just the Talk: Becoming Your Kids' Go-To Person about Sex* (Minneapolis: Bethany House, 2015), 52.

6. McAfee, "America's Youth Admit to Surprising Online Behavior, Would Change Actions If Parents Were Watching," June 4, 2013, www.mcafee.com/us/about/news/2013/q2/20130604-01.aspx.

7. Arialdi M. Miniño, "Mortality among Teenagers Aged 12–19 Years: United States, 1999–2006," Centers for Disease Control and Prevention, May 2010, www.cdc.gov/nchs/products/databriefs/db37.htm.

8. Centers for Disease Control and Prevention, "Youth Risk Behavior Surveillance—United States, 2015," *Morbidity and Mortality Weekly Report* 65, no. 6 (June 10, 2016), www.cdc.gov/mmwr/volumes/65/ss/pdfs/ss6506.pdf.

CHANGE 4: PRESS PAUSE

1. Michelle J. Watson, "The Father Wound of Anger," *Shaunti Feldhahn: Research, Insight, Hope*, December 4, 2014, www.shaunti.com/2014/12/father-wound-anger/.

2. Willard F. Harley Jr., *Love Busters*, rev. ed. (Grand Rapids, MI: Revell, 2002), 99.

3. Edward T. Bedford, *Bits & Pieces*, September 15, 1994, 11–13.

CHANGE 5: SEGUE

1. Andy Stanley, North Point Web interview, posted February 13, 2015, https://vimeo.com/120401973.

2. David R. Smith, " 'Can I Have a Phone?' Answering Every Kid's Burning Question," June 8, 2016, www.thesource4ym.com/youthculturewindow/article.aspx?ID=328.

3. "What Age Should My Kids Be before I Let Them Use Instagram, Facebook, and Other Social Media Services?" Common Sense Media, accessed August 17, 2016, www.commonsensemedia.org/social-media/what-age-should-my-kids-be-before-i-let-them-use-instagram-facebook-and-other-social#.

CHANGE 6: ADD A QUESTION MARK

1. Alexandra Samuel, "Parents: Reject Technology Shame," *Atlantic*, November 4, 2015, http://www.theatlantic.com/technology/archive/2015/11/why-parents-shouldnt-feel-technology-shame/414163/.

2. Paul Kent, *The Real Force: A Forty-Day Devotional* (Franklin, TN: Worthy Inspired, 2015).

3. Michele L. Ybarra, Victor C. Strasburger, and Kimberly J. Mitchell, "Sexual Media Exposure, Sexual Behavior, and Sexual Violence Victimization in Adolescence," *Clinical Pediatrics*, June 13, 2014, doi: 10.1177/0009922814538700.

CHANGE 7: WALK WITH

1. "The End of Absolutes: America's New Moral Code," Barna, May 25, 2016, https://barna.org/research/culture-media/research-release/americas-new-moral-code#.V7R_OI-cFPa.

2. American Academy of Pediatrics, "Children, Adolescents, and the Media," *Pediatrics* 132, no. 5 (November 2013), http://pediatrics.aappublications.org/content/pediatrics/132/5/958.full.pdf.

3. Caroline Knorr, "7 Media-Savvy Skills All Parents Need in 2014," January 4, 2014, Common Sense Media, www.commonsensemedia.org/blog/7-media-savvy-skills-all-parents-need-in-2014.

4. Mahatma Gandhi, quoted in Frank Raj, "Gandhi Glimpsed Christ, Rejecting Christianity as a False Religion," *Washington Times*, December 31, 2014, www.washingtontimes.com/news/2014/dec/31/gandhi-glimpsed-christ-rejecting-christianity-fals/.

WHAT NOW? 25 WAYS TO APPLY WHAT YOU'VE JUST READ

1. Jonathan McKee, *52 Ways to Connect with Your Smartphone Obsessed Kid: How to Engage with Kids Who Can't Seem to Pry Their Eyes from Their Devices!* (Uhrichsville, OH: Shiloh Run Press, 2016).

2. Jonathan McKee, *The Guy's Guide to God, Girls, and the Phone in Your Pocket: 101 Real-World Tips for Teenage Guys* (Uhrichsville, OH: Shiloh Run Press, 2014).

3. Jonathan McKee, *Sex Matters* (Minneapolis: Bethany House, 2015).

TURN THE PAGE TO READ
AN EXCERPT FROM

Author Jonathan McKee offers just the help you need to have meaningful interaction with your kids instead of always overreacting to their unhealthy consumption of technology and media. In a world where over 80 percent of 12- to 17-year-olds now own a smartphone, parents are searching for ways to pry their kids' eyes from their devices and engage them in real, face-to-face conversation. McKee—drawing from his 20-plus years of experience working with teenagers, studying youth culture, and raising three teens of his own—provides an abundant supply of useful tips and creative ideas to help you bond with the Smartphone Generation.

Being Smarter
Than the Smartphone

"I can't get my daughter to look up from her phone and actually talk with me."

I hear this almost every weekend as I finish teaching one of my parent workshops. Moms and dads approach me and ask me how to connect with their tech-obsessed kids. Not so coincidentally, I'm experiencing the same struggle with my own kids. The smartphone is becoming a growing source of frustration, vying for everyone's attention.

Two hours later, I'll speak to a room full of teenagers. As I hang out with them afterward, inevitably I'll hear, "My mom and dad don't understand. All they do is nag me all the time. It's not like I'm out dealing drugs or driving drunk!"

It's interesting being in the unique position of hearing regularly from parents and from teens. Week after week, I hear the same thing. Parents regularly complain, "My kids spend too much time staring at their stupid phones!" And teenagers always protest, "My mom and dad won't let up about my phone!"

So who is right?

Last month my youngest daughter asked me honestly, "Dad, you don't think I spend too much time on my phone, do you?"

She had heard all the hype about "too much time on screens." You probably have too:

- *Today's thirteen- to eighteen-year-olds spend about nine hours (eight hours, fifty-six minutes) on entertainment media per day, excluding time spent at school or doing homework.* Common Sense Media did the extensive research in 2015. When you add up the time today's teens devote to TV, music, social media, video games, and all the personal time on their mobile devices, the numbers add up to more than a full-time job. And guess which device they're clocking the most hours on?

- *Screens hinder sleep.* In a recent study by the National Sleep Foundation, more than half of parents said their fifteen- to seventeen-year-olds routinely get only seven hours of sleep, or less, though the recommended amount for teens is eight and a half to ten hours. Why? Sixty-eight percent of these teens keep an electronic device on all night.

- *Screens can make your grades drop.* A brand-new study by Michigan State University followed five hundred MSU students, monitoring their academic performance as professors competed with smartphones, laptops, and other devices to get participants to engage. "The more they relied upon their gadgets as a distraction—even if it was to undertake quasi-relevant activities such as reading the news—the further their grades fell," the study states.

- *Screens are a new playground for bullying.* Gossip has just been given a turbo boost. Roughly 43 percent of teens have been harassed online (with about 25 percent of them claiming to have suffered more than one instance of it). Girls are twice as likely to be victims of cyberbullying, compared to boys, and, sadly, they are twice as likely to commit it, as well. Not surprisingly, kids who've endured cyberbullying are much more likely to attempt suicide than those who haven't. And parents are overwhelmingly unaware of the harassment their kids suffer. Studies have uncovered a rather large gap between kids' experiences and parents' perception. While at least one-third of students are frustrated by the reality of cyberbullying, a mere 7 percent of parents say they're worried about it affecting their children.

- *Screens create a pressure to be liked* in a world where many females already feel self-conscious about their looks. In fact, some researchers studying this struggle to keep up the perfect image online have observed low self-esteem, loneliness, and deep levels of unhappiness as a direct result of using the web. *A growing number of teenagers use screens for sexting.* Researchers from Drexel University recently surveyed college students, asking them if they had ever sent or received "sexually explicit text messages or images" when they were under age eighteen. Fifty-four percent said yes.

- *Screens provide so many distractions, experts now claim kids shouldn't own them until they are thirteen years old.*

So is this just a bunch of helicopter parents worrying too much, or are some of these legitimate concerns?

Let me come clean.

If I am being completely honest, I'd have to say that a smartphone can be a help or a hindrance. It just depends on who owns whom.

A phone can be a remarkably valuable tool. Let's face it: all the people who wrote those articles mentioned above warning us about the dangers of the overuse of smartphones and social media own smartphones. I own a smartphone. I love it. (I just recently used it to find out the name of the song playing in a restaurant—thanks Shazam!)

So when does tech become a hindrance?

The answer is simple: tech is a great tool, but a lousy crutch. The moment we all become socially dependent on tech. . .Houston, we have a problem.

"Think about it," I challenge teenagers at school assemblies, "how many times have you sat in a circle of your friends and none of them is talking because their heads are all down staring at their phones?"

Students always laugh and point to each other: "That's so you!"

Smartphones can sometimes distract us from the person sitting right in front of us—often a person we care about far more than the endless stream of posts we're scrolling through at the moment.

Don't get me wrong: I believe smartphones can actually help people enhance their personal relationships. Think about how you use it. While eating your breakfast, you can see the new baby pic your best friend posted from a different state. You can text your kids from work to tell them what time you're picking them up. You can call your spouse while driving home. Phones can actually help us connect.

But tech becomes scary when it's our primary source of interpersonal communication. Reason being? Tech actually can hinder normal face-to-face communication.

I've been researching youth culture and technology for decades, and I've encountered countless studies about young people spending too much time with technology. I keep using the word *technology* simply because, if your kids are like mine, then they aren't just staring at their phones, they are also clocking in hours looking at other screens. Even today's video game systems offer interactive and chatting components. All over the country, teens and tweens are sitting in front of TV screens, wearing headsets, and talking with people they've never even met face-to-face as they explore a virtual world together. This may scare parents on many levels, but one by-product of all this screen communication is that the more time young people spend communicating via texting and IM, the less they recognize real-life face-to-face social cues.

For example, in 2014 UCLA did an eye-opening study in which they observed kids who were unplugged and media-free for five days at an outdoor camp. By the end of the five days, these kids were better able to understand emotions and nonverbal cues than kids who were plugged into a normal media diet.

What does this mean? It simply suggests that real-life, face-to-face conversations are superior. Yes, even when we use "emojis"—part of the digital slang of the new millennium—digital communication isn't as powerful as good ol' fashioned face-to-face.

Similarly, researchers witnessed this reality clearly in a bonding experiment in which people engaged in conversation with friends four different ways: in person, and through video chat, audio chat, and instant messaging. As you can probably imagine, bonding was measured and differed "significantly across the conditions." The greatest bonding occurred during the in-person interaction, followed by video chat, audio chat, and then IM, in that order. Good ol' fashioned face-to-face communication always wins.

When today's young people focus on digital connections as their primary social connections, the results are always negative. Research shows that many young people today base their own self-worth and value on online affirmation. The result is too much time trying to impress an online audience and a decline in intimate friendships. In other words, many young people today are substituting true friendships with online "friends."

This even has ramifications in the dating world. A new study by researchers at Stanford and Michigan State found that couples who met online are less likely to stay together long term than those who meet off-line.

So how can parents help teenagers swing the pendulum back toward real-life, face-to-face connections?

Tech Enabled

We need to help teenagers move from being *tech dependent* to *tech enabled*. Phones are really convenient tools for helping us communicate with people *outside the room*, but they become a hindrance when they interfere with our connection with people *inside the room*.

In my "How to Be Smarter Than Your Smartphone" school assembly, after hashing through many of these realities with teens, I always challenge them:

> If Mom or Dad accuses you of spending too much time with tech, don't argue. Instead of getting defensive, just prove it with your actions. Slide your phone into your pocket, go hang out with your friends, and talk with them face-to-face. In fact, try this:
>
> - Log off social media for a day and just hang with your friends outside.
> - Go on a kayak ride with that girl/guy you talk with so well.
> - When you see that beautiful sunset, resist the temptation to snap a pic, find the perfect filter, caption it, and post it on Instagram. Instead, just enjoy the sunset! Maybe even look up and thank the Creator of that beautiful scene. Then pull out your phone and text your mom, telling her when you'll be home.
>
> Tool—yes!
> Crutch—nope.

So I ask you, as a parent reading this book, which of these are you modeling?

Our kids will never learn how to be responsible with their phones if we ourselves are slaves to our own devices. It doesn't matter how many lectures we give or how hard we try to teach what we know; we can only reproduce who we are.

I need to hear this just as much as anyone else. As a parent of three, I've failed at this countless times and am regularly learning hard lessons. (I should be brilliant by now, with all the mistakes I've made!) And that's the key: learning from our mistakes, letting them make us better, and then adjusting our behaviors. I call this "adaptive parenting."

As parents, we have the unique opportunity to demonstrate how to use technology responsibly and effectively. As imperfect humans with a phone in our pocket, we can model how to responsibly use our devices for entertainment, for knowledge, and as a tool for connection. More importantly, we can show them how easy it is to actually turn off the TV, set our phone or tablet aside as we enter the dining room, and enjoy a meal together uninterrupted. We can easily keep our phone in our pocket when we're hanging out with friends. We can turn it off when we go away on a three-day camping trip—where we're without a Wi-Fi signal—and actually survive!

This book is full of ideas that may help families look up from their devices and enjoy face-to-face relationships.

Before Diving into This Book

As you read through these fifty-two ideas, you're going to start noticing some common denominators. In fact, some people may be tempted to discount some of them and say, "Eating a family dinner is pretty much the same thing as taking your daughter to coffee!" I'd be quick to reply, "Yes, and taking your kid hunting is really similar to going on a bike ride. They're both outdoor activities that catalyze a climate of continuous conversations." (Nice use of alliteration, huh?) But you'll find these common denominators quite necessary—*and extremely helpful*—for two reasons:

1. ***Each of these ideas presents unique characteristics and advice.*** In both the "Two-Player Mode" and the "Netflix-Binge Bonding" chapters, you'll notice each setting involves parents actually using technology to connect with their kids. Similarly, you may notice several chapters helping you use questions to engage kids in conversation ("Fingertip Questions," "The *My Big Fat Greek Wedding* Method," et al.). Each of these chapters will provide new tools you can use for these specific situations. Besides. . .

2. ***Your kids' tastes are going to vary.*** One kid may really respond to late-night splurges but may never be interested in stopping for frozen yogurt on the way home from school. Another may be open to no tech at the table but would freak out at the mere suggestion of a media fast, especially regimented No-Tech Tuesdays. If your kids are like mine, they'll be unique in taste and temperament. The more ideas you have in your arsenal, the better.

So enjoy these ideas, most of which I've drawn not only from years of research, but also from my years out on the front lines as an imperfect parent who wanted to connect with his kids. These are many ideas that worked for my wife and me. I hope some of them will be a help for you as well.

The Coviewing Connection

Way back in 2004, I read about a California mom who learned the hard way that she didn't know as much about her kid as she thought she did.

Roberta "Bobbi" MacKinnon died from injuries after being flung from a playground merry-go-round propelled by a rope tied to the back of a vehicle. Bobbi and her friends had watched the MTV show Jackass and decided to try to copy their merry-go-round stunt. The result was fatal.

I read about the story in my local newspaper. Joan MacKinnon, Bobbi's mother, said, "I had no idea that she watched the show. Maybe I would have made her stop and think that this is dangerous fun."

I clearly remember my reaction reading Bobbi's mother's words that day. I swallowed hard and thought, That could be me! I don't know every show my kids watch.

In the silence of the moment, I heard the TV on in the other room. I thought, Oh great! My kids are watching something right now, and I don't even know what it is!

I popped up from my chair and ran into the other room. They were watching the cartoon *SpongeBob SquarePants*.

As I stood there in the doorway, I recalled a study I had just read in the journal *Pediatrics,* revealing the importance of parental guidelines with entertainment media. One of the techniques the authors suggested was "coviewing"—simply sitting down and watching entertainment media with your children so you can use it as an opportunity to talk about important family values.

So I sat down and watched *SpongeBob* with my kids (and found it quite hilarious. . .especially that Patrick!).

In a world where we are constantly at battle with kids and their screens, coviewing can be a really fun practice where you join them enjoying screen time. After all, we're talking about a lot of screen time per day.

The screen today's teenagers stare at more than any other is that small one they carry around with them in their pocket. In fact, according to the Common Sense Media report I cited at the beginning of this book, teens spend two hours, forty-two minutes per day on their smartphones alone, then one hour, thirty-seven minutes on a computer, and another one hour, thirty-one minutes watching TV. That's just the "average kid." So your own kids may spend more or less time on these devices. And you can be sure that if your daughter doesn't watch ninety-one minutes of TV per day, she has a friend at school who is more than making up for it in her home.

The point I'm making is this: use some of this screen time as a point of connection.

No, coviewing is not the most social activity you can do as a parent, but it accomplishes two tasks:

1. ***It gives you a peek into their world of entertainment media.*** What shows do your kids watch? What online videos do they frequent? What is the content of all this entertainment? What lessons are they walking away with after watching it? Many parents have no idea what kind of entertainment their kids are consuming on their screens. Do you?

2. ***It provides you with a springboard for conversations about what you just watched.*** When a major character makes a decision, simply ask your kids a question when the show is over. "Was he right?" Sometimes

that simple three-word question can spark a debate between siblings where all you need to do is sit back and eat popcorn while they do all the talking. Other times it may necessitate asking more questions to provoke further discussion. Don't feel the need to discuss everything you watch. This will quickly grow tiresome. But don't hesitate to jump on occasional opportunities.

Coviewing opens up a host of possibilities for conversation.

No, I'm not endorsing watching just anything with your kids. If you begin watching something with your kids and it is completely against your family values, then it's your job as a parent to say, "Sorry, kids, we aren't going to watch this." Or, better yet, ask them, "Kids, do you think we should watch this? Why not?"

Avoid overreaction. If you freak out every time you sit down to watch something with your kids, they're going to hide from you and only watch TV at their friends' houses. Make these coviewing connections a pleasant experience. Discover fun shows that you all enjoy watching together.

By the way, coviewing can be done on any size screen, not just on the fifty-five-incher in your living room (more on that later).

So look for those opportunities to simply enjoy some entertainment together. This practice can provide fun bonding times and sometimes a good springboard for conversation.